Southward Bound

*The adventure and wonder
of road trips through Latin America*

David Miller

© 2024 by David Miller

All rights reserved. No part of this book may be reproduced or transmitted in any form or by any means, electronic or mechanical, including photocopying, recording, or by an information storage and retrieval system, without permission in writing from the publisher.

Scripture quotations are from
The Revised Standard Version of the Bible
© 1971 and 1952.

ISBN 979-8-218-53789-0

Cover design: JD&J Design

Photos by David, Benjamin and Molly Miller, Lindsey Croasdale and Jonathan Todd.

Printed in the United States by IngramSpark

To the many Latin Americans
along our route who taught us
the true meaning of hospitality

Books by David Miller

The Lord of Bellavista
The dramatic story of a prison transformed

The Path and the Peacemakers
The triumph over terrorism of the church in Peru

Song of the Andes
The impact of the gospel on the Andean peoples of Bolivia

To Russia, With God's Love
When the Cold War yielded to the Prince of Peace
(With Mark Shaner)

Available in paperback or Kindle versions. More information at DavidMiller220.com

Chapters

1. The very idea *U.S.A* 1
2. The silence in Mexico *Mexico* 6
3. Mount Mary *Mexico* 12
4. Chiapas *Mexico* 18
5. Volcanoes *Guatemala* 26
6. The land of the Savior *El Salvador* 32
7. Honduras in a hurry *Honduras* 40
8. Heroes *Nicaragua* 46
9. Pura vida *Costa Rica* 54
10. The world's crossroad *Panama* 61
11. Pearl of the Caribbean *Colombia* 67
12. Medellin *Colombia* 74
13. The Bolivarians *Venezuela* 82
14. Amazonia *Brazil* 91
15. Endless in Brazil *Brazil* 98
16. Big water *Brazil-Argentina* 106
17. Hunting ground *Argentina-Paraguay* 114
18. Home in the Llajta *Bolivia* 122
19. Sites unseen 132
20. Patagonia *Argentina* 133
21. Atacama Desert *Chile* 141
22. Inca Heartland *Peru* 149

The very idea

Homer Firestone is to blame for putting the idea in my head.

We were in my pickup truck one day on our way to some place in the Andes when Homer spotted an old jeep he had once driven from California to Bolivia and began reminiscing about the overland trip. Until then, I had never heard of such a thing. As a rookie missionary I had a difficult time wrapping my head around the concept.

Understand, the distance between my stateside residence in Indiana and my home in Cochabamba takes 10 hours to cover in a jet airplane flying 550 miles an hour in a straight line. I could not fathom making the journey over the squiggly roads running every which way over the maps of Central and South America.

Then there were the security questions. Homer made the trip in the 1960s, when the territory between Mexico's Rio Grande and Cochabamba's Rio Rocha was more or

The very idea

less peaceful. Corrupt policemen, greedy border officials, petty thieves and voracious mosquitos were the most serious dangers he faced.

But in the 1970s, violent civil wars flared up across Central America. A decade later, guerrilla armies controlled much of rural Colombia and Peru. One of their favorite military tactics was to throw up random road blocks to rob or kidnap unsuspecting travelers.

I put the notion of an overland trip to South America out of mind. Barbara and I were now the parents of four kids and international travel had become a complicated endeavor. Our lifestyle dictated that we spend one year of every five in Indiana, so we made regular trips between Bolivia and the U.S. But the prospect of doing it with small children in tow by any means other than a jet plane flying in a straight line was unthinkable.

Nevertheless, the idea of an overland trip had lodged itself in an obscure corner of my brain and sometime in the early 2000s it suddenly resurfaced. I decided we had to do it, and soon.

Mark Twain is to blame for jarring the idea loose. One day I came across a quote from the renowned author. "Twenty years from now, you will be more disappointed by the things you didn't do than by the ones you did do," Twain said.

I could think of a lot of things I regretted not doing and I decided this was not going to be one of them. I started talking the idea up to Barbara around the time our youngest daughter Carmen left for college. We were suddenly empty nesters, and international travel had become less complicated.

By this time, Central America had long been at peace, Peru's once dreaded Shining Path had self-destructed. The Colombian government had brokered a peace treaty with its long-standing rival, the Revolutionary Armed Forces of Colombia (FARC). Except for the brutal drug cartels operating near the Mexican border, the road from Hoosierland to Bolivia lay open and untroubled.

Barbara eventually agreed, though with some trepidation, mostly because of the Mexican cartels. It seemed that whenever we mentioned the plan to friends and family, they also brought up the question of the cartels. Everyone except our son Ben and daughter Molly. They both were graduating college that year so we invited them to come along. They didn't think twice before signing on.

With savvy advice from some experienced Mexican travelers, we came up with simple strategies to evade the cartels. (Not to worry, I will happily reveal those tips with you once we get down there.) That left us to solve the final piece of the puzzle: how to convince our boss to approve the plan. For this, I had to come up with a more compelling reason than Twain's warning of regrets 20 years down the road.

My original rationalization for the trip was identical to Homer's. I would buy a cheap used car in the U.S. and drive it to Cochabamba to save the shipping charges. The reduced import duty on a used vehicle would save us even more money. Barbara and I would end up with a good, dependable vehicle on the field for a fraction of the usual cost. It simply made good financial sense.

But this plan fizzled when Bolivia's new president, Evo Morales, decreed that cheap used cars could no longer be imported to Bolivia. My good-financial-sense argument evaporated overnight.

In the spring of 2009, Barbara and I were driving across Nevada in our 1996 Toyota Camry when another idea popped into my head. We would drive this aged car as far as the Panama Canal, give it away, and

The very idea

make the rest of the trip on public transportation. Of course!

But now we had to come up with a new argument for our boss to approve the trip. One factor in our favor was our new job as Regional Coordinators for Latin America. The position had expanded our field of service out from Bolivia to everything between the Rio Grande and Tierra del Fuego.

So, I composed bullet points to demonstrate how the trip would strengthen our relationships with church leaders in the countries in route. We could get better acquainted with one another and organize cooperative projects.

The experience would deepen our understanding of Latin America's numerous sub-cultures and update us on social issues. We could investigate, up close and personal, emerging opportunities for church planting and disciple making. In short, we could see firsthand what God was doing and how our missionary role could better fit His Plan.

God had certainly been doing something extraordinary in Latin America. British sociologist David Martin published a ground-breaking book in 1990 entitled *Tongues of Fire: The Explosion of Protestantism in Latin America*. His research revealed that 400 Latinos were turning to Jesus every hour. We wanted to witness where, why and how this remarkable growth was taking place.

Our boss approved, albeit with some reluctance. So, on September 19 we gave our infant grandson one last squeeze, rolled out of our Indianapolis driveway in our aged Camry and headed south. Friends at our first overnight stop in Lexington,

Kentucky, laid hands on the vehicle and invoked God's protection over the car and its passengers.

Their prayers were answered. During the entire 12,500-mile, three-month odyssey, we did not once see the inside of an emergency room or a police station. That kind of safety record comes only through divine intervention.

We saw other unmistakable signs of divine intervention along the way. As we shared the daily life of Latin Americans, we enjoyed like never before the continent's immense beauty and warm and welcoming inhabitants. Everywhere we looked, we saw fascinating opportunities to fit our missionary role into God's Plan. The journey indeed turned into a once-in-a-lifetime experience. Ben and Molly still refer to the trip as "The Epic."

Really? you might ask. If that be true, what's all this stuff about dictators and drug traffickers and poverty and crime in Latin America? Where's the beauty in that?"

Good point, and one that I can't answer in just one chapter. You will have to come along on our epic journey in order to examine the evidence. I would like to show you what we discovered, from travel tips to must-see natural wonders to unexpected miracles, large and small.

But if you do come, I must warn you of a serious danger. The journey just might persuade you to do that thing you've been thinking of doing, but haven't done, for the past 20 years.

The silence in Mexico

On September 23, 2009, we crossed the border between McAllen, Texas, and Reynosa, Mexico, leaving Anglo America behind for our southward trek across Latin America.

If you watch the news nowadays, crossing the Mexican border appears risky. It was not then. Nevertheless, I was nervous. Would Mexico allow our aging Camry, well past the point of obsolescence, into their country?

My worries were unfounded. Mexican officials processed the paperwork, sold me the mandatory travel insurance and had us on our way within 20 minutes. This would prove to be the most expeditious border crossing on our entire route.

However, we still had to evade the scrutiny of crime rings and Mexico's fabled police force, the *Federales*. Cartel operatives reportedly scout gringos crossing the border to gage if their cars are worth hijacking. They especially covet late model 4WD drive pickups and SUVs with plenty of horses under the hood in order to outrun the Federales.

I was betting that the bad guys would not take a shine to our worn sedan with its double-digit horsepower and more than a quarter million miles on the odometer. The Federales could easily outrun this car, on foot if they had to.

My calculations must have been correct. Neither cartel operatives nor the Federales bothered us on the four-hour drive to our first overnight stop in Saltillo.

A key travel tip from some friends from Ohio helped us here. A couple years prior, they had driven a used van across Mexico for delivery in Guatemala. Ohio does not require license plates on the front of vehicles, as Mexico does. Police officers would see them coming and know instantly that they were foreigners. Our friends were pulled over about three times a day, on average, and seldom got away without paying some kind of "tip."

At their suggestion, I color-photocopied my Indiana license plate, laminated it with plastic and bolted it to the front of the Camry. I'm fairly confident this was the reason we made it through the entire country without once paying tips to the Federales.

It actually took surprisingly little time for my nervousness about motoring through Mexico to subside, due in large part to our encounters with ordinary Mexicans. Attentive customer service and laid-back hospitality took on whole new meanings. Mexico is one of the most user-friendly countries you will ever visit.

Pemex station attendants not only pump your gas, but ask to check your oil and tire pressure while they're at it. At one restaurant stop, we couldn't find a dish we wanted on the menu. "But I will be glad to make it for you," the cook said cheerfully, and did.

The silence in Mexico

A family in Jalapa we had never met paid for our night's hotel stay in that charming city, along with meals, taxi fare, ice cream and cappuccino. They did this simply because we were friends of friends. Friendship in Mexico, no matter how distant, comes with privileges.

Finally, we found that the world's largest Spanish-speaking country has a lot of attractions for the traveler. These include stunning scenery, alluring beaches, outdoor symphonies in town plazas, sumptuous food and archeological wonders.

One unique Mexican phenomenon is invisible to the naked eye. Somewhere south of Saltillo you cross an unmarked boundary into a region that social researchers have dubbed the Circle of Silence. The Circle stretches from San Luis Potosí to Michoacán and from Querétaro to Guadalajara.

Mind you, Mexico's heartland bustles with industry, agriculture, ranching, tourism and culture. The Circle is certainly not silent in that way. The researchers call it the Circle of Silence because of a spiritual void they have discovered there.

The data reveals that the population of the Circle is less than one percent "Great Commission Christians." Commonly called *evangélicos* in Spanish, they are identified as born-again followers of Jesus committed to leading the kind of life He did and making more followers of Jesus as He instructed them in the Great Commission [See Mathew 28.18-20 and Acts 1.8].

Their absence here is astonishing. First, because no other area of Latin America today contains so few committed followers of Jesus. On average, one of every five Latin Americans is a Great Commission Christian. In some places, they are more plentiful. Brazil, the region's largest country, is 27 percent evangelical. Great Commission Christians comprise 25 percent of the population of Puerto Rico, the nation with the highest quality of life index. [Source: Operation World].

The Circle of Silence is an even more astonishing phenomenon when you take into account that, up until 1950, all of Latin America was like the Circle, nearly devoid of evangélicos. Then the movement began to grow, first moderately, then beginning in the 1970s, explosively. Everywhere, that is, except in the 115 counties of Mexico within the Circle of Silence. Evangelicals here are still the tiny minority they were a century ago.

This is not due to lack of effort. Disciple makers and church planters are actively engaged in the Circle of Silence, despite hardship and lack of interest on the part of locals.

Take my friends Miguel and Esperanza. The couple met and married in Nueva Italia, a small city in the state of Michoacán. They then headed north to Saltillo to study in a Bible Institute. Upon graduation, denominational leaders offered Miguel a position as pastor of an established congregation on the U.S. border. The job came complete with a steady salary, free housing, an automobile and prestige.

Miguel declined. "God called me to plant churches," he explained, "not to be the pastor of somebody else's legacy church."

"But this church needs a pastor," church officials insisted, "and it needs one now."

"Yes, but Michoacán needs churches," Miguel countered. "There are lots of churches here in the north. I must go where that need is greatest."

"That's too bad," they said. "If you decline our offer, you will be on your own. We have no budget to plant churches in Michoacán."

Miguel and Esperanza returned to Nueva Italia to plant churches. It was tough going. They both worked secular jobs to support the family. They raised their two children in two windowless rooms on the first floor of a building that eventually would house the first congregation they launched.

By the time they moved to Mexico City years later, the couple had planted seven churches in Michoacán. When they assumed leadership of a large church in the nation's capital, Miguel, ever one to grow new things, set about cultivating a hydroponic garden on the chapel rooftop. Once a planter, it seems, always a planter.

The new ministry did not mean the couple was finished in the Circle of Silence.

"We are not just planting churches, but also starting schools in Michoacán," Miguel explains. "If we don't reach the children now with the gospel, they're going to grow up and work for the drug cartels. Many of them already are, because they see that as their only option."

Miguel once took me to visit Nueva Italia and, like all small cities in Mexico, I found it a charming place. Once word got around that Miguel was visiting from Mexico City, friends showed up to deliver an impromptu serenade in his honor.

The singers had come to know Jesus under the influence of Miguel and Esperanza, I learned. They also told me that city fathers had once bestowed a good citizen award on the couple because of their positive impact on the community.

Most of the Great Commission Christians I know who are planting churches in the Circle of Silence are like Miguel and Esperanza. No fanfare, no big budgets, no lavish auditoriums. They live a simple, sacrificial lifestyle while quietly persuading friends and neighbors to follow Jesus.

In recent years, some of these church planters have formed a mission cooperative to focus attention on the task. They call it, appropriately, Good News for the Circle of Silence.

This is very good news indeed for Mexico. History shows that, once the Good News arrives and takes root in an unreached part of the world, it inevitably breaks the silence.

Mount Mary

When we arrived in Bolivia three months after leaving Indianapolis and having traveled through 12 Latin American countries, I asked Ben and Molly this question: "If you had the chance to return to any place we visited on this trip, which one would you choose first?"

Without hesitation they both said, "Why, Mexico, for sure."

The primary reason for their selection, they said, was the food.

Of course, you cannot go to Mexico and not eat tacos. *Taquerias* are everywhere, offering infinite varieties and variations of this staple of the Mexican diet. We attempted to try them all, which admittedly would take several lifetimes.

Mexicans eat *tacos al alambre, tacos al pastor, tacos de carnitas, de bistec, de cabeza, de milanesa, de camarón, de pescado* . . . well, you get the picture. Pardon the Spanish names, but these tacos really have no equivalent in English.

I should point out that I have never eaten a taco in Mexico made with hamburger meat and iceberg lettuce, primary ingredients of Tex-Mex tacos common in the U.S. Perhaps this explains why Mexicans and gringos seldom see eye-to-eye on so many other issues.

This is not to say that tacos are the only thing you will find on the menu in Mexico. It is said that the country boasts of more than one thousand national dishes, no two alike. Every city and region claims its particular specialty.

For example, one of Monterrey's finest restaurants is famous for goat, and offers little else to its upscale clientele. Five-star hotels in Acapulco feature lavish breakfast buffets complete with highly skilled omelet chefs, all included in the price of your overnight accommodation.

A friend in Saltillo treated us to mouth-watering *borrego al ataud*, lamb slow-roasted in a wooden box served with only soft corn tortillas and chili sauce, the one vegetable dish consistently served with Mexican meals.

Should you tire of tortillas, you can always shop one of Mexico City's self-service French bakeries and take home an assortment of breads from among the dozens of warm and delectable selections continuously rolling out of the ovens.

Mount Mary

You must try one example of genuine Mexican ambrosia, the *Enchilada En Nogada*. A roasted poblano chili is stuffed with a blend of chopped meat, pecans, apples and dried fruit, and smothered in creamy pecan gravy. Pomegranate seeds and cilantro are sprinkled atop the enchilada to represent the colors of the Mexican flag.

Not only is it delicious, but patriotic as well. Enchilada En Nogada is purportedly the specialty of Puebla. Nevertheless, I recommend you experience this dish wherever and whenever you come across it, which is typically in the month of September when Mexico celebrates its independence.

I wrote earlier about Mexico's warm and friendly hospitality, and I suspect that was the second reason Ben and Molly wanted to return. In fact, I suspect the food in Mexico is exceptionally delicious because of the congenial surroundings in which it is served.

No place have I experienced more warm and friendly hospitality than in Monte Maria, a Mexico City neighborhood whose name literally translates as "Mount Mary." It is home to a charismatic megachurch with a fascinating history. An elder told me the story once on a drive from the airport to the congregation's guest house in Mount Mary. Some highpoints:

On April 25, 1979, Roman Catholic priest Aurelio Gomez Velazquez was attending a clergy conference when he heard for the first time that God is love. The revelation stunned him. His religious training to that point had painted God as strict, stern and judgmental. Never had Gomez heard anything that led him to believe that God loved him.

14

"I prayed to God in the mighty name of Jesus and was born again," the priest said. "His spirit came upon me as in the Upper Room."

Gomez accepted water baptism and began to talk to his congregation about what he called his transformation to a new life. His parishioners noticed an unmistakable change in their priest and a powerful quality to his preaching. Many repented and experienced God's love and forgiveness themselves.

One day Gomez invited them to join him to pray for the sick in what he called an Assembly of Health. Seventeen persons attended the first assembly held in a small chapel of the Alamedas Catholic Church. A few experienced healings and told friends and family about the miracles. Word got around. Soon, hundreds of sick people inundated the streets of the affluent Alamedas borough. The municipal council asked Gomez to move the Assembly of Health to a different venue.

So, in 1982, Gomez led what he called "the exodus to the Mount." The congregation began worshipping outdoors on 7.5 acres in the Monte Maria neighborhood. So many people came to hear Gomez preach, they soon filled up the space.

The priest then found a 250-acre tract known as El Nogal in the cool, arid mountains northwest of the city. Gomez began organizing outdoor prayer, praise and healing meetings there. These events attracted crowds estimated at 200,000. "The field at El Nogal was one of the great experiences of faith," Gomez said.

The priest's activities eventually sparked backlash from his superiors. A bishops noted that Mount Mary Church had dispensed with images and confession booths. In place of the Eucharist, Sunday worship consisted of praise music, prayer and Bible preaching.

His presiding bishop finally delivered a three-point ultimatum to Gomez. If he wanted to remain a priest, he was to rename Mount Mary Church "Our Lady of Health", turn over El Nogal to the diocese, and sever all fellowship with Protestant Christians. Gomez declined, effectively renouncing his priestly office. He did it, he said, "In the full possession of my mental, intellectual and moral faculties, and in the name of our Lord Jesus Christ."

Mount Mary

When Gomez announced to his congregation that he no longer belonged to the Catholic Church, attendance dropped precipitously. Only about 500 worshippers showed up the following Sunday, leaving thousands of unfilled seats in the outdoor esplanade. Mount Mary Church would have to rebuild.

One day in Mexico City's central market Gomez encountered a man who would help do that. An American missionary named Robert Stevenson was expounding the Bible to passersby. Gomez was attracted to the fellow's passionate preaching and asked Stevenson if he would come work with him at Mount Mary. The young American agreed.

Stevenson's path to Mexico had begun some years before in a U.S. prison. He once mentioned to me why he was in jail, but I can't remember the details. Anyway, they are not important. Stevenson was just out of his teens when some Christians visited him behind bars and explained how he could follow Jesus. Robert decided to do that and his life took a radically new direction.

Upon his release, Stevenson began preaching the gospel himself, tutored by the same Jesus followers who led him to Christ. Not long afterward, he met Bonnie, a beautiful young woman with red hair, an engaging smile and plenty of street smarts of her own. They married and sometime later answered God's call to the mission field.

Robert and Bonnie saw that calling fulfilled at Mount Mary Church. In 2006, just weeks before he passed away from pulmonary fibrosis, Aurelio Gomez and church elders commissioned Robert as the new pastor of Mount Mary. By then, the church had rebounded to several thousand members.

If you visit Mount Mary Church on a Sunday, you will experience buoyant gospel music, fervent prayer and Bible-centered teaching. And after worship, you can treat yourself to a gourmet meal at the congregation's open-air restaurant.

This is not an exaggeration. Mount Mary's lead chef formerly trained apprentices to work in five-star hotels in Acapulco.

He once told me had earned a phenomenal salary doing this, but struggled with alcohol abuse. His career nosedived. Then he met Jesus, stopped drinking and began living a simpler but more rewarding life. Mount Mary employed him to supervise its food service, as well as the kitchen at Hacienda El Nogal. Now a rustic rural conference center, El Nogal hosts several international gatherings each year.

I have been privileged to attend two of these events myself and can't wait for an opportunity to return. Food is not the only allure, but it is a primary consideration. (Hint: the guacamole alone is worth the trip.)

Hacienda El Nogal serves up Michelin class food with that warm hospitality you come to expect in Mexico. And yet, there is something about its meals that is novel, fresh, almost exotic.

In fact, you might say that the food is simply out of this world.

Chiapas

You can easily drive a private vehicle from Mexico's northern border with Texas to its southern border with Guatemala in three days. We took more than 10, meandering along a less than straight line to see sights and rendezvous with friends.

Mexico has the greatest number of World Heritage Sites in the Western Hemisphere. Even though we saw only two--Mexico City's famous Socalo and the magnificent ruins of

Southward Bound

Teotihuacan—we needed extra time to do so.

I should mention that our rule of thumb was to be off the road every day by sundown, when magnificent sights disappear in the gloom and driving hazards proliferate. I would recommend that any gringo venturing across Mexico in a private automobile observe this rule.

While we're at it, here's another travel tip. If given the option, always take one of Mexico's excellent private toll roads. Some can be a little pricey, depending on how long they have been in service, but these thoroughfares will always get you where you want to go in considerably less time.

One caution however. Always look both ways when changing lanes on private toll roads. Friendly as they are, Mexicans do not always obey posted speed limits.

Several days spent in Mexico City added to our commute across the country. A local church hosted us in a comfortable downtown hotel, giving us time to explore a tiny sampling of the plazas, parks, museums, monuments and markets in this amazing metropolis.

Greater Mexico City's population of 22 million places it at number five among the world's largest urban centers and in continuous competition with Sao Paulo, Brazil, for title of the largest in the

Chiapas

Americas. Both are ranked well ahead of New York and Los Angeles, the two biggest metro areas in U.S.

Once you head south from Mexico City and drop off the central highlands, the weather grows increasingly warmer and the vegetation lusher. When you reach Chiapas, the most southern of the United States of Mexico, you realize you are most certainly in the tropics.

Before you cross into Guatemala you must pass through the Chiapas Highlands. Pine forested hills that arise from torrid jungles to altitudes exceeding 9,000 feet, the Highlands remind the traveler of the Smoky Mountains in some places, the Ozarks in others. But the tile-roofed farmhouses and tiny plots of corn, beans and coffee squeezed together across the landscape reminds one that this is still Mexico.

I had looked forward to introducing Barbara, Ben and Molly to the Chiapas Highlands. This was the part of the country I had most often visited as a news correspondent reporting on abuses of religious liberty. Chiapas is home to Mexico's second largest population of native Americans. And as happens with indigenous people groups across the globe, they have suffered more than their share of abuse.

The town of San Cristobal de las Casas, the state's first capital until supplanted by Tuxtla Gutierrez, is still considered the cultural capital of Chiapas. Its narrow streets are lined with quaint shops and homes, and lead to pleasant plazas and charming colonial churches.

Outdoor markets are resplendent with colorful clothing, blankets and ponchos sewn and sold by native artisans. Rustic cafes abound that brew locally grown coffee and sell freshly roasted beans. My favorite brand? *Café David*, natch.

By far the largest municipality in the Highlands, San Cristobal is surrounded by hundreds of small villages where Tzotil- and Tzeltal-speaking farmers practice a way of life essentially uninterrupted for millennia. Closer in, the town is ringed by makeshift suburbs. These are refugee settlements, in fact, for evangelical Christians. San Cristobal de las Casas' suburbs are stark witness to some of the most violent and relentless abuse of religious rights in the Americas.

When Spanish colonials introduced European political order and the Roman Catholic faith to Mexico in the 16th century, restless tribes in the Chiapas highlands rebelled, fighting several indecisive wars with Mexico City. *Caciques* (community chiefs) were determined to preserve both their local political power and ancient Mayan religion.

When the last war with the federal government ended in a stalemate in the late 1900s, Chiapas caciques were granted *de facto* rule. In exchange for delivering votes to the ruling political party in national elections, the caciques were granted total autonomy to rule local townships.

Unfortunately, the cozy political relationship did little to raise the quality of life for native Americans in Chiapas. Illiteracy is well above the national average and household income well below the poverty line.

Caciques have adamantly clung to ancient Mayan religious practices, worshipping the sun and earth, and practicing animal sacrifice. These customs eventually fused with Catholic dogma to produce a Christo-pagan rite known today as Traditionalist Indian Catholicism.

San Juan Chamula, the second largest town in the Chiapas highlands, lies six miles from San Cristobal de las Casas. It is both the caciques' political headquarters and the primary shrine of Traditionalist Indian Catholicism.

I have visited the town several times, but only once ventured inside the Traditionalist temple of San Juan Chamula. Heavy darkness immediately enveloped me upon entering, even though hundreds of candles burned on the altars. Stern statues of unnamed saints lined the smoky walls. I stepped over piles of pine branches, wild grasses and cut flowers, and took note of small animals and chickens awaiting ritual

Chiapas

slaughter. The sensation was not one to lift my spirit heavenward.

In 1920, evangelical Christianity was first introduced to the Chiapas Highlands by Presbyterian missionaries José and Luz Coffin. They found indigenous farmers eager to receive the gospel. Within five years, the Coffins had planted three churches, organized six primary schools and opened a Red Cross office. They needed help.

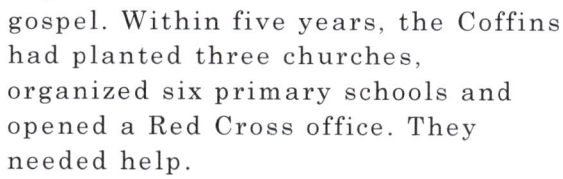

John and Mabel Kemper from the Reformed Church of America responded to their plea. John bought the first automobile available in Tuxtla Gutierrez and drove it to San Cristobal de las Casas when a new road opened to the Highlands. The new faith began to spread even more rapidly through the small villages and tile-roofed farmhouses.

Serious conflict with Traditionalist Indian Catholics flared up almost immediately. Caciques realized, and rightly so, that Bible-based Christianity was a serious threat to their political and spiritual monopoly. They responded with violent persecution that would last for more than six decades and produce Mexico's largest population of religious refugees.

By the 1990s, caciques had driven nearly 40 thousand Tzotzil and Tzeltal farmers off their ancestral lands because of their refusal to renounce their Christian faith. Most took up residence in the makeshift suburbs on the outskirts of San Cristobal de las Casas, scratching out a living as street vendors, day laborers or domestic servants.

Salvador Lopez is one of them. His story, though extraordinary, is not atypical of his neighbors who decided to follow Jesus.

Salvador recalls the early morning in August 1976 when a drunken mob surrounded his family's house in Toltzeman. "Get ready," they shouted, "we're taking you to San Juan Chamula by order of the caciques."

His parents told the 19-year-old to take with him his most prized possession, a guitar. They knew the mob would not let the family return to retrieve belongings. "You play so well," they said. "It would be a shame to leave it behind."

The Lopezes were among 35 Christian families rounded up that morning. When the assembly arrived at San Juan Chamula, caciques told them that they could never return to their homes and farms. If they tried, they would be beaten, jailed, or perhaps killed.

One of the caciques spotted Salvador's guitar and snatched it from his hands. "This yours?" he asked mockingly. Then he smashed the instrument to pieces on the street. Literally with just the clothes on their backs, the refugees made their way to San Cristobal de las Casas.

Salvador began to search house to house for work to support his wife Veronica and the couple's new baby. It was slow going. He could not speak Spanish and knew only how to farm corn and beans. Because of their decision to follow Jesus, Salvador and Veronica faced years of poverty. They eventually settled in Nueva Esperanza, "New Hope" in English, a neighborhood established especially for Christian refugees.

The couple's hardships were light compared to some. In July 1981, six men abducted Miguel Gomez Cashlan, the founder of Nueva Esperanza. Angered by his compassionate support of fellow Christians and incessant gospel preaching, the band gouged out Cashlan's eyes, cut out his tongue and scalped him before hanging him by the neck. Only one of the assassins was ever brought to trial. He spent eight years in jail for the grisly murder.

In November 1997, assassins using high-powered rifles ambushed and killed religious liberty activists Salvador Collazo and Marcelino Perez. A coroner reported 16 bullet wounds in Collazo's body. He left behind a young widow and four small daughters. Although witnesses could identify the murderers and gave their names to police, the investigation into the murders was delayed for months and ended indecisively.

The Constitution of Mexico declares that "every person is free to profess the religious beliefs that please him or her." This article evidently does not apply to Christians in the Chiapas Highlands. Whenever it suits their purposes, caciques disregard the constitution and break the law with impunity.

Yet despite exile, poverty, wrongful imprisonment and death, Native Americans in Chiapas have embraced the gospel of Jesus in record numbers. A survey of non-Catholic Christians in Mexico shows just how remarkable their commitment to Jesus has been. By the decade of the 1990s, evangelical Christians were roughly 11 percent of the general population of Mexico. But in Chiapas, a state plagued by the most relentless and violent persecution in the Americas, evangelicals were 38 percent of the local population.

Salvador and Veronica Lopez have been part of that growth. For 10 years after their expulsion from Toltzeman, Salvador supported his family by working construction and dedicated his free time to itinerant preaching. Eventually he left the construction trade and assumed leadership of The Divine Savior Presbyterian Church in Nueva Esperanza. His congregation grew to over 1,000 members and planted five other churches among exiled Christians in other towns.

As I mentioned, Salvador's story is extraordinary but not atypical. The Presbyterian Church in Chiapas grew from zero to over 85 thousand members in its first 40 years. At this writing, Chiapas Presbyterians comprise 800 thousand of the estimated two million Jesus followers in the state. The movement started by the Coffins and the Kempers is so strong, in fact, that foreign workers are no longer necessary. The last Reformed Church of America missionaries withdrew from Chiapas in 2015.

The ancient church father Tertullian observed that the blood of martyrs is the seed of the church. My journalistic career reporting on the persecuted church has consistently reinforced that observation. Nearly everywhere in the world that Jesus followers are threatened, beaten, jailed or assassinated for their faith, the church grows unchecked.

At first glance, this seems a puzzling outcome. But when you think about it, isn't this exactly the outcome we should expect from the One who laid down his life for his friends?

Volcanoes

The road drops several thousand feet over a relatively short distance from the Central Highlands of Chiapas, Mexico, to the Guatemala border below. I confess I don't recall a lot about this leg of the trip, but our son Ben does. He recently shared this page from his diary describing that day's drive:

"We follow a river through dense forestation, wild flowers and thick greens engulfing the narrow road in deep shade. Then suddenly a spot opens on the side of the road and we can see the thousand-foot plunge to the water below. We climb and climb, snaking up steep grades, then descend in controlled chaos, like a pinball making its way down an obstacle course.

"As if this were not enough, we have to contend with the most brutal speed bumps known to humanity. Mexicans call them *topes*, Guatemalans know them as *tumulos*. These are not the only inconsistencies. One town has planted fortresses in the middle of the road. Other bumps have been worn down to near oblivion. Some are painted hues of yellow that warn of their severity, others are camouflaged in shady spots to deliver harsh blows to the bottom of cars. We must have gone over 200 or more of these things in less than 60 miles.

"We suffered some snags at the border crossing and night fell before we entered Guatemala. Under the cover of darkness, it was impossible to discover these rough hurdles until an instant before plowing into them.

Brakes squealed in attempts to prevent us from separating the chassis from the rest of our overfilled auto. The ride was a rollercoaster, and how we emerged at the other end with no flat tires and all parts of the Camry still intact is a miracle to me."

[*Editor's note: This is an abridged version of Ben's diary page. I confess to deleting some of the more, um, startling parts.*]

His mention of "some snags at the border crossing" deserves elaboration. If you should ever make a trip like this, you might encounter pleasant, smiling young men on the side of the road offering to help you navigate a border crossing for a small fee. Never, NEVER under any circumstances, accept their "help".

I cannot for the life of me remember why I did. Maybe my nerves were still jangling from the startling descent from the Chiapas Highlands. Maybe I was in a generous mood and keen to give enterprising youth some honest employment. Maybe I just zoned out and momentarily lost my mind, losing contact with reality, as well. To be honest, this is exactly what happened.

Volcanoes

Every seasoned traveler knows that these pleasant young men do not seek honest employment, nor do they render help to the poor dupes they manage to bamboozle. They are, in fact, the world's most effective rip-off artists and you should treat them as such. Do not speak to them, do not make eye contact, and DO NOT give them anything, not even the time of day.

Me, well, I gave them everything they asked for: their entire fee, in advance, and our passports. I was smiling pleasantly all the while.

As I said, I had momentarily lost my mind.

The pair disappeared into the line of waiting vehicles and did not reappear until two hours later. They explained in hushed tones that a problem had arisen and they needed more money. If we wanted to proceed into Guatemala or ever see our passports again, we would have to fork over more cash.

I won't recount all the disgusting details about what happened next. You only need know that a border crossing that should have taken us 20 minutes stretched into more than six hours and sucked up about 10 times the standard fees. Needless to say, nobody was smiling when it was over.

But we did finally enter Guatemala, at night, and picked our way over a dark highway riddled with maddening tumulos, now invisible to the naked eye. We somehow made it to modest motel where we fell into bed with no supper.

The next morning dawned bright and sunny. We greeted a group of friends from Florida who were staying at the same modest motel. Then we were off on our way across Guatemala, the land of volcanoes.

It seemed like the entire time we traveled through the country we were never out of sight of a perfect, conical peak on the horizon. Just as one picture-perfect volcano passed out of view behind us, another magnificent specimen appeared in the windshield.

Yet, there was one stretch when the volcanoes disappeared altogether. That was during a steep climb through thick clouds up to Lake Atitlan. The fog was so dense we could barely see the roadside until we emerged in the dusky sun to see Atitlan itself. Said to be the world's most beautiful crater lake, it is ringed with, you guessed it, volcanoes.

During our visit there, Barbara took an excursion across the lake with Benjamin to visit an innovative school his college buddies had told him about. The trip took most of a day, the only way to get there being by boat. Much of the entire north shore of Atitlan is inaccessible by road due to the volcanoes.

If Atitlan is one of the world's most beautiful lakes, then Antigua is certainly one of its most beautiful cities. Nestled in the enchanting Ponchoy Valley, Santiago of the Knights of Saint James, the town's official name when founded in 1543, served for two centuries as the seat of Spanish Guatemala, a colony that included all of present-day Central America and the Mexican state of Chiapas.

It was not the colony's first capital city. That one was buried by volcanic debris from the nearby Volcán de Fuego (Volcano of Fire). Antigua was positioned outside the reach of these destructive "lahar" flows, but nevertheless suffered devastating earthquakes with alarming regularity. The evidence of these tremors is apparent in Antigua's architecture. The walls of its colonial buildings are built of six-feet-thick masonry.

Following a particularly destructive quake, Antigua finally had to relinquish its status as the seat of government to a city built on safer ground and christened New Guatemala, the present-day Guatemala City.

Volcanoes

Guatemala is the largest country in Central America by population (18.3 million), of which nearly half (43.43% to be exact) are of native Mayan or Xinca descent. And while Spanish is Guatemala's official tongue, 42 different languages are spoken within its borders. It is Central America's most indigenous country.

We believe that is why Guatemala feels so familiar to us, because we reside in South America's most indigenous country, Bolivia. Indigenous peoples comprise 36.8% of its population and speak 36 different languages. We concede that Bolivia boasts far fewer volcanoes. However, the largest of them, Sajama, rises to 21,463 feet, the highest point in the country. Ah well, enough competitive banter.

Although Roman Catholicism has been the dominant religion in Guatemala since the arrival of Europeans, as is true in all Spanish America, the spiritual environment of the country has changed considerably since the first evangelical Protestant missionary arrived in 1882. For example:

> One in four Guatemalans today professes to be a born-again Christian, making it one of the countries with the highest percentages of evangelicals in all Latin America.

> Aided by several new translations of the Bible into indigenous languages, church-planting movements are thriving among ethnic Mayan peoples.

> The nation-wide Evangelical Alliance calculates that there are more than 40,000 churches in Guatemala. If this statistic is correct, it means there are 96 evangelical congregations to every one Catholic parish in the country.

> The Christian Fraternity of Guatemala, commonly known as the Mega Frater Church, has seen its

attendance grow from 20 at its founding in 1979 to more than 20,000 today. It is the largest Pentecostal congregation in Guatemala and meets in one of the largest church buildings in the world.

> Two past presidents, Efraín Ríos Montt and Jorge Serrano, were outspoken about their evangelical faith while in office. Both generated serious political crises that forced them out of office before completing full terms.

> Researchers report that Guatemala's Roman Catholics and evangelical Protestants share their faith more than citizens of any other country of Latin America.

> Explosive growth of the Orthodox Church is taking place among the ethnic Mayan peoples, prompting bishops to migrate there from Eastern Europe.

Such is the complex, dynamic, unpredictable growth of Christianity in this culturally diverse nation. And though I still feel Guatemala seems a familiar place to me, I confess that these developments among its Christian community are, to put it mildly, surprising.

Perhaps such surprising developments stem from Guatemala's vast cultural diversity, or its intricate social fabric. Maybe economic imbalances have triggered unexpected results. Yet, I suspect it might have something to do with geography.

After all, if you stop to think about it, your approach to life and God and eternal destiny just has to take on a heightened sense of urgency when you live among volcanoes.

The land of the Savior

At the border crossing between Guatemala and El Salvador an immigration official confused Ben with Molly. Which was which? she demanded to know, glancing between the photos in their passports and the two look-alike siblings standing before her.

Our kids' hairstyles triggered her puzzlement. Ben wore long, thick dreadlocks cultivated during his college years. Molly, on the other hand, had shorn her luxurious blond tresses and sported the GI Jane look. She claimed the new style attracted less unwelcome attention from strangers and would be easy to groom during months of travel through the tropics.

It took some earnest explanation to convince the suspicious border official that the youth before her with the masculine haircut was a young woman and the other with hair spilling to the shoulders was a young man, and that neither was trying to disguise his or her identity. With a weary sigh, the officer stamped entry visas into their passports.

My memory may fail me here, but I don't recall hearing the customary, "Welcome to El Salvador," as she pushed the documents across her desk at us.

So, welcome to El Salvador. In English, "The Savior," a country literally named for Jesus.

Any nation that carries such a name would be hard-pressed to live up to it. El Salvador tries, and fails, like every earthly nation will, to achieve the standards of justice, peace and happiness that its Namesake established for His Kingdom (See Romans 14.17). El Salvador dreams, like all nations do, of one day achieving something great.

Granted, El Salvador is not large in the territorial sense. It has been dubbed the "Tom Thumb of the Americas." The country measures only 170 miles from east to west and 90 miles north to south. It is smaller than every state in the U.S.A. except Connecticut, Delaware and Rhode Island.

Personally, I think of El Salvador as the Mighty Mite of Latin America. It exerts a regional influence much greater than would be expected of a nation-state its size, thanks to its skilled labor force, strategic geographical location and diversified economy. A business-friendly environment has created innovative homegrown enterprises and attracted multinational companies. The country maintains the second highest level of income equality in Latin America, a key factor in sustaining a stable middle class.

These benefits have not come without pain and suffering. Along with the rest of Central America, El Salvador won independence from Spain in 1821 and, like much of the region, endured political instability and social inequality for the next century and a half. Persistent unrest finally led to a 12-year civil war. The conflict erupted full-scale on March 24, 1980, when a right-wing death squad shot and killed popular Archbishop Oscar Romero as he was saying Mass at the altar of a church.

By 1992, when President Alfredo Cristiani and the commanders of five guerrilla armies signed a peace treaty at Chapultepec Castle in Mexico, more than 75,000 Salvadorans had perished. Thousands more had been "disappeared" by the brutal death squads. The Chapultepec Peace Accords effectively ended the vicious cycle of violence and established a multiparty constitutional republic. Salvadorans found grace to bury the hatchet and embrace national reconciliation. Unlike many nations that have experienced violent struggle, the

The land of the Savior

country rebounded from the ravages of war in remarkable fashion.

When we arrived in the capital city of San Salvador we received the warmest of welcomes from our hostess, Suzy Garcia, and her family. Business owners and active members of an evangelical church, they hosted us with kind and casual hospitality during the week we spent in their home.

As any proud Salvadoran would, Suzy immediately served up *pupusas*. If you have never had the pleasure, you might have a hard time imagining the pupusa, or comprehending the passion this delicacy inspires in Salvadorans. You take a thick, puffy tortilla, split it lengthways and stuff it with salty cheese, *chicharron* (crispy fried meat), squash, refried beans, buds of the *loroco* plant, or all of the above.

Pupusas are typically served with tomato salsa and *curtido*, a cross between German sauerkraut and Korean kimchi. The Pilpil people who invented the pupusa consider it a sin to cut tortillas with a knife, so Salvadorans are careful to eat their national dish with the fingers. They have also declared the second Sunday of November "National Pupusa Day."

When it comes to food, it doesn't get any more passionate than this.

Our 2009 visit was not the first time Suzy and family hosted the Millers. Ben had spent a week at the Garcia home during his senior year in college while conducting research for a thesis. That investigation focused on El Salvador's present national conflict: violence perpetrated by the *Mara Salvatrucha*.

Ben briefed us on the history of the notorious criminal gang and details of the story surprised us. Foremost is that Mara Salvatrucha, also known as M-13, was made in the U.S.A.

In the 1980s, Salvadoran families began migrating in ever increasing numbers to southern California to escape the bloody civil war. Many young men were among the refugees. At home, they risked forced recruitment into guerrilla groups fighting the government, or else forced recruitment into the army to fight the guerrillas.

The newcomers found Los Angeles particularly inhospitable. The city's resident outlaw gangs made life harsh for the immigrants, to the point that young Salvadoran men found it necessary to organize their own gang to protect themselves.

They chose the name "Mara," some observers say, as homage to La Mara Street in San Salvador. "Salvatrucha," it is believed, is a combination of "Salvadoran" and "trucha," a word that means "be alert" in the Caliche slang spoken in the country.

Regardless of where the name came from, it inspires fear and repugnance in El Salvador, Guatemala and Honduras, countries where the gang primarily operates.

Following the end of the 1980s war, gang members returned to El Salvador in quantity. Some came by choice. Others arrived after being arrested for crimes committed in the U.S. and summarily deported. Once established in Central America, Mara Salvatrucha began to build wealth through extortion, soliciting "protection money" from local business owners. Those who refused to pay, risked assassination.

The land of the Savior

On our way through Guatemala City, we saw a newspaper report about a driver and his assistant dragged off their public bus and murdered in front of the passengers. The bus owner had not paid protection money. The newspaper report noted that, in the first eight months of that year, 157 bus drivers and conductors had been similarly murdered.

It so happened that the large evangelical church we visited on our one Sunday in San Salvador was holding its inaugural service in a new downtown sanctuary. The congregation had relocated to the heart of the city from its original neighborhood under duress, so the celebration was tinged with certain melancholy.

The pastor told us that, the church had long operated a bus for parishioners who needed a ride to worship services. Then, M-13 demanded protection money for the bus to continue using the route through its turf. When the money was not forthcoming, gang members waylaid the bus and held up passengers at gunpoint, twice. Ridership plummeted.

"I went to the M-13 commander and asked him to give us a break," the pastor said. "'After all, we are a church,' I told him. 'We don't charge a fare. In fact, it costs us to operate the bus.'"

"He answered with a shrug. 'Sorry, can't do that. If I let you off the hook, my superiors will simply kill me and put somebody else in my place. I will be dead and you will still have to pay.'"

Mara members become well acquainted with violence, beginning

36

with initiation into the gang. When they agree to join, recruits endure a vicious pummeling by veteran members. The excruciating welcome serves to test their loyalty and seal their bond with fellow Maras. It must work. Few gang members abandon the ranks once initiated.

In actual fact, loyalty is strictly enforced by the threat of death. The gang insists on lifetime commitment and exterminates those who leave early. Ben learned that gang rules allow only two acceptable motives for resigning: marriage and religious conversion.

Gang leaders profess to respect just two things in this world, God and family. So, if a member wishes to depart in order to marry, he may do so. However, the gang monitors his behavior and if he cheats on his wife or abandons her, he is killed.

Should a Mara profess Jesus as savior, he can also petition for discharge. If his testimony appears genuine to the Mara leadership, permission is granted. Again, the gang remains watchful. Should the convert backslide, say by forsaking worship services or going on a drinking binge, he is killed.

As a journalist reporting news about Christians living in areas of conflict, I have been privileged to interview some true heroes of the Faith. I met several of them in El Salvador. The men and women who risk their lives every day to make disciples of Jesus among the

The land of the Savior

Mara Salvatrucha and its rival gang, Barrio 18, are that class of heroes.

Ben became acquainted with gang evangelists while doing his research thesis and introduced us to some of them. One remarkable young man had recently moved his wife and children from Los Angeles to San Salvador in answer to God's call. Another gospel worker, Saul, is a chaplain and educator in a prison populated by Mara inmates. Abner, one of his colleagues, was shot and killed by the gang three weeks after we made his acquaintance.

While writing this chapter, news about gang activity in El Salvador appeared on the BBC. The most alarming story reported that 62 persons were killed, allegedly at the hands of MS-13 and Barrio 18. This happened in a single day: Saturday, March 26. Ominously, it was the most violent 24-hour period in the country since the end of the civil war in 1992.

The victims included the pastor of an evangelical church in San Matias who was gunned down in front of his young son. The motive of the shooting was unknown at press time.

The BBC also carried a video report* about another evangelical pastor. Entitled "God or the gang," it documents the work of Will Gomez, a gang member turned Jesus-follower. He leads Ebenezer, a church full of men and women who have left gang life to serve God.

"The gangs know what we believe, they follow what we do," Gomez says on camera.

"But we have traced a line of respect. 'This is God's Kingdom,' we say. 'We don't get involved in your business, don't get involved in ours.'"

So far, the line of respect has shielded Pastor Gomez and his flock from gang attacks. He estimated that 50 men had passed through his rehab program since it was first established. Of those, 30 have remained faithful to Jesus. Of those who did not, five are now dead.

As expected, loyalty was strictly enforced.

Welcome to El Salvador, a land of suffering and beauty, tragedy and promise, conflict and joy. A land where, every day, people make choices that lead to life or death.

Welcome to a land not so much different from your own.

_____

Produced by Wietske Burema and first published on BBC News 26 July, 2019.

Honduras in a hurry

Although Honduras is the second largest country in Central America, we spent the least amount of time crossing its territory than of any of the 12 nations on the Epic itinerary. Our aged Camry made it from border to border in a mere two and a half hours. This was on purpose.

We wanted to get through Honduras ASAP. This was partly on account of gun violence. Hondurans own a lot of firearms and too often use them to settle disputes. We had heard verifiable accounts of drivers shooting it out with one another following traffic mishaps. We did not want to get caught in the crossfire.

We also knew of travelers waylaid by armed assailants intent on hijacking their automobiles. One friend managed to speed away from one such assault, but lost an eye in the process.

Another deterrent to a long visit was the reputation of the national police for exacting hefty payments from foreign motorists for traffic violations, real or contrived. I admit that I did not verify whether or not the reputation was warranted. The probability of it being so was reason enough.

The final argument for a

swift crossing was the state of Honduran politics at the time. Two months before our arrival, a *coup d'état* had ousted leftist President Manuel Zelaya. The prior year Zelaya had joined the ALBA alliance, a group of anti-Yankee-imperialist states such as Cuba, Venezuela and Nicaragua. When Zelaya proposed alterations to Honduras's constitution, he was promptly ousted by conservatives who sensed he was trying to perpetuate his regime indefinitely as had, well, the presidents of Cuba, Venezuela and Nicaragua.

We had no strong opinion on the country's politics, and still don't. Nevertheless, we knew that civic unrest translates into protests, general strikes and road blocks. We did not want to get caught in the crossfire.

We could scoot across this sizeable country in a couple of hours because the Pan-American Highway crosses Honduras at its narrowest point. The north coast stretches for 400 miles along the Caribbean Sea, but from there the country's borders taper down like the sides of a triangle to a tiny stretch of Pacific Ocean at the Gulf of Fonseca. Our route skirted the Gulf in a direct line between El Salvador and Nicaragua.

Please do not conclude that our hasty passage suggests that Honduras holds no allure for the traveler. One can find many good reasons to spend time here. For example, Honduras shares, with Mexico, Guatemala and Belize, the world's second largest coral system. More than half of the 600 mile-long Mesoamerican Barrier Reef lies off the north shore of Honduras, attracting divers from around the world.

Near its western border with Guatemala sits the ruins of the Mayan city of Copan. A certified archeological wonder of the world, Copan is still rendering secrets of ancient America to historians and anthropologists.

There are the several tracts of virgin jungle that beckon erstwhile eco-tourists. The largest of these, the Platano River Biosphere, covers a whopping seven percent of the total territory Honduras. Finally, have you ever heard of or read about or watched the movie starring Harrison Ford about the notorious Mosquito Coast? Guess where it stars. Yep, that's right.

Honduras in a hurry

In case you are traveling to Honduras by private auto, I should mention that the first 50 feet of the trip took us twice as long to negotiate as the rest of the distance across the country. This was due to a four-hour procedure required to move our aged Camry across the border from El Salvador to Honduras.

Yes, four hours. It went like this.

We arrived at the customs house to find no Honduran officer on duty. He strolled in 20 minutes later for his shift, which had started 40 minutes earlier. Go figure.

The task of examining and stamping my customs papers apparently exhausted him because he disappeared midway through to take a coffee break. He returned a half hour later just as his young female assistant reported for work. They greeted one another with a long and passionate kiss while I waited before the officer's desk. For several minutes, the couple was oblivious to both me and the clock.

The clock showed that an hour had passed since I first stood before the officer. No noticeable progress had been made on my paperwork. The officer told me that I should go to another office, get a paper and bring it back to him. He would stamp that paper so that I could take it to one of the several banking kiosks that surrounded the customs parking lot and pay the duty on our car.

I did this, or at least attempted to, but then discovered that none of the kiosk windows were open. I returned to the customs house and shared this piece of news with the officer. He said, well of course the banks are closed because today is a holiday in Honduras.

I did not ask him the obvious question, which was, of course, "Why the heck did you send me to pay my fees if you knew the banks were closed?" That, I am certain, would have dragged out the process yet further.

Instead, I gritted my teeth and murmured, "So, what shall I do now, sir?"

He suggested two options. One, I could wait until the banks opened the next day. Right. "Or you can leave your paperwork with me with money for the fees, plus a modest commission, and I will take care of it first thing tomorrow."

That is how, at the very outset of my hurried crossing of Honduras, I was taken for a ride.

Please understand, not all Hondurans are out to dupe the stranger and take his money. As in most nations of the world, the vast majority are honest, hard-working people. Nevertheless, there are a few bad apples among them. Just as the adage predicts, a few can spoil the whole bunch.

This may partly explain why Honduras suffers from horrendous social inequality and economic underdevelopment. According to government stats, two out of three Hondurans live below the poverty line. One in five survives on less than $2 a day. Two hundred rural Hondurans leave their home communities every day in search of a better life. They seldom find it. The communities they leave behind typically suffer more social decline and poverty after their departure, and become resigned to a future marked by scarcity, violence and depression.

In 1989, a college professor from Florida and former Peace Corps volunteer named Charlie Smith decided to do something to reverse the rural exodus. His vision began to take shape in a "model village" he built in a secluded valley in the Lake Yojoa region. There, Smith began to conduct research and teach seminars.

His experiments and their practical application focused on improving agricultural methods, upgrading community infrastructure, delivering adequate health care, developing markets for local goods and, most basic of all, teaching the Bible and encouraging Hondurans to become serious followers of Jesus.

Smith's vision mobilized local churches to serve the poor with Bible-based solutions to their everyday needs. Theologians today refer to this as a "holistic" proclamation of the gospel. The idea has been around for some time, actually. Legend has it that St. Francis of Assisi, who died in 1226, was asked by his followers how they were supposed to carry on his work. "Go preach the gospel," he replied. "If you have to, use words."

Smith called his vision "Heart to Honduras." The organization soon began attracting volunteer teams of engineers, contractors, doctors, nurses, homemakers, and college and high school students to Honduras for one- to three-week stints to learn about community-based development and do what they could to help.

From the get-go, Smith insisted that his coworkers see Hondurans as capable, competent colleagues. He believed that every community, no matter how poor, possessed the resources necessary to improve quality of life. His aim was to help rural families develop "adequate and sustainable income" that could keep them together on their farms. This, in turn, would reduce flight to large cities and foreign countries.

On its website, Heart to Honduras expresses the organization's vision in these terms.

"We see young people with a future."

"We see heroes who are writing beautiful stories of belonging, hope, dignity, and endless possibility."

Smith understood that this sort of transformation takes time. Changes in the way people think, work and organize their affairs do not happen overnight, even with the light of the gospel showing the way. It was going to cost Smith a lot of time--a lifetime, perhaps--to see his vision through. So, he built living quarters at the model village to spend plenty of time every year in Honduras.

Sadly, time ran out for him before he saw his vision grow. Smith contracted pulmonary fibrosis and died at age 59, only eight years after founding Heart to Honduras.

Someone has said that there are two kinds of people who leave their mark on the world, heroes and hero makers. Charlie was a remarkable example of the second kind. He managed to instill his vision in coworkers who have carried on the work in remarkable fashion. Today Heart to Honduras is not only going strong, but expanding its work with innovative ideas and immensely useful projects.

Many of the engineers and college students and doctors and nurses who contribute their time and money to rural Honduras have likely never heard of Charlie Smith. His name rarely comes up anymore in conversations in the model village he built. Many thousands of rural Hondurans who are living Charlie's vision of community life have no inkling about the man who came up with the idea originally.

But I don't think he minds. Hero makers, it turns out, more interested in making a difference than in making a name.

Charlie Smith is buried on a mountain overlooking that secluded valley in the Lake Yojoa region. As the old song says, he left his heart in Honduras.

It's obvious that he was in no hurry to leave.

Heroes

Two young policemen in Nicaragua served us the one and only traffic ticket we collected on the entire Epic journey. Well, not quite. The junior officers only threatened us with a traffic ticket, which they offered to waive if we paid them a courtesy fee.

It happened like this. As we pulled out of the first small town we encountered after crossing the border, we found ourselves in the midst of a line of cars. Ben was at the wheel. As the line of cars accelerated, the junior officers waved ours over to the berm.

It was only then that I noticed their radar gun. They said that we had exceeded the speed limit by 15 kilometers per hour. Since we had seen no speed limit signs anywhere, I had no way of knowing if that was true or not. But I hesitated to argue with a cop holding a gun.

Instead, I remarked that if we were speeding, then the other cars in the line were speeding as well. Why did they not stop them?

They glanced at each other from behind their dark sunglasses, before one said, "Well, we can't catch everybody."

That is true, of course, and I assume explains why policemen invariably stop cars with foreign license plates. I mentioned this possibility to the officers, who glanced at each other again. An uneasy silence followed, perhaps because they didn't expect a car with foreign license plates to talk back to them in Spanish.

One policeman stepped forward and said, in a slightly conciliatory tone, "Look, ordinarily we would take you back to town to pay a fine in front of our captain. But since you are foreigners, we are willing to settle this here and now."

He then named his price. We had no way of knowing if the amount, somewhere between $10 and $15 U.S., was more or less than the fines paid in front of his captain. Of course, compared to the fine I once had to pay to a rude state trooper on the Pennsylvania Turnpike who also had a radar gun and a keen eye for out-of-state license plates, this was peanuts.

But then, any fine seems stiff when one is innocent, or at least no guiltier than others. I protested mildly, not because I thought it would do me any good, but in the hope that a bit of righteous indignation might save a fellow motorist from paying a courtesy fee in the future. I handed over the money and we were on our way.

If you should ever find yourself in a situation like this, take solace from a wise lawyer I know. "Don't forget, the cost of living in Latin America is low," he told me. "After all, where else in the world can you buy a cop for just ten bucks?"

I could write a lot of things about Nicaragua. Central America's largest country by land mass, it boasts the sub-continent's largest inland body of water. Lake Nicaragua is home to a rare species of freshwater sharks. The country produces excellent coffee and is the birthplace of one of my best friends. * But first impressions are powerful and even now years later, that threatened traffic ticket still stings.

One cannot write about Nicaragua without mentioning Sandino. He is the country's recognized national hero. Like many a national hero, he lived a shorter-than-average life span and met a tragic end.

Augusto C. Sandino was born in 1895 as the illegitimate son of a wealthy landowner and his indigenous servant girl. He was raised by his mother until age nine, when his father took him into his home to educate him.

At age 26, he nearly killed the son of another prominent citizen after the young man insulted Sandino's mother. The incident forced his exile to Mexico, a country then in the throes of a radical revolution. There Sandino was exposed to the ideas of anarchists, mystic gurus, communists and the Seventh-day Adventist church.

Core ideas of the Mexican Revolution left the biggest impression on the exile, however. Ideas like the separation of church and state, equitable land reform, the right to vote and fair wages. Sandino witnessed firsthand the formation of a new "institutional revolutionary" government that introduced a sweeping array of political and social reforms to Mexico.

Sandino returned to Nicaragua in 1926 and soon launched his own revolution. A civil war had erupted between the Conservative and Liberal political parties and Sandino joined the Liberal camp, rising to the rank of general. His side was on the verge of victory when a powerful foreign government intervened and forced his fellow commanders to sign a peace treaty.

Sandino considered the treaty a sham and refused to lay down arms. Instead, he retreated into the bush with soldiers under his command and launched a guerrilla war against the foreign occupation force that now policed Nicaragua.

That force was the United States Marine Corps and Sandino would fight them for the next six years. The U.S. government branded him a "bandit", the equivalent of being placed on the list of Designated Foreign Terrorists today.

Many of his fighters wielded only machetes against their well-armed foe. Casualty counts in early battles were 20 to one in favor of the Marines. But try as they might, the Marines could not kill or capture Sandino. Eventually, his exploits earned him an international reputation as a kind of Central America Robin Hood.

Sandino never came close to a military victory over the Marines, to whom he referred as "foreign invaders". But history was on his side. When the Great Depression hit, the United States could no longer afford to maintain troops in Nicaragua. Franklin Roosevelt withdrew the Marines in 1933 as part of his recently enacted Good Neighbor policy.

On February 21, 1934, Sandino traveled to Managua to meet with newly elected president Juan Bautista Sacasa. The two were well acquainted. They had fought together in the 1926 civil war and both had declined to sign the peace treat brokered by the U.S. In the meeting, President Sacasa agreed to grant amnesty to Sandino, provide land for his fighters and build schools for their children. In exchange, Sandino pledged his loyalty to Sacasa.

Upon leaving the presidential palace, Sandino and his contingent were waylaid by members of the National Guard, a military police force trained by the departed U.S. Marines. Soldiers took the men to an isolated area on the city fringe,

Heroes

executed them and buried their corpses in unmarked graves.

Sandino was 38 years old.

Anastasio Somoza, another of Sandino's comrades in arms during the civil war and newly appointed commander of the National Guard, had ordered his murder. Betrayal did not stop there. A year later, Somoza staged a *coup d'état* against Sacasa. The commandant subsequently ascended to the presidency himself and used the office to establish a family dictatorship that would last for more than 40 years.

When Somoza was assassinated in 1956, the presidency passed to his eldest son, Luis. Luis died of a heart attack in 1967 and was succeeded by his younger brother, Anastasio Somoza, Jr. A popular uprising finally unseated the last Somoza in 1979. He fled the country for Paraguay, where he was assassinated the following year.

The rebel movement that overthrew the Somoza dynasty named itself after Sandino. Known as the Sandinista Front for National Liberation, it claimed to uphold the legacy of Nicaragua's tragic hero. It seemed as if Sandino's ghost had returned to exact vengeance.

Other than his name, however, today's Sandinistas have little in common with Augusto Sandino. Daniel Ortega, guerrilla commander turned politician, has clung to the presidency for some 20 years by manipulating sham elections and brutally repressing dissidents. His grim record of corruption and human rights abuse equals, or exceeds, that of the Somozas.

Sandino, of course, is still revered in Nicaragua. In 2010, Congress unanimously voted him a National Hero.

While on the subject of heroes, I could not write about Nicaragua without mentioning Bill.

Managua was an important stop on the Epic journey and Bill was the first person we connected with upon arrival. He was helping us organize an international forum of Kingdom workers in a pleasant retreat center in the mountains near the Pacific coast. Bill was good at stuff like that. He knew a lot of people.

Well over six feet tall with broad shoulders, shaved head and an iron grip, Bill was a bear of a man, someone you could easily mistake for a former professional wrestler. I recall feeling a bit intimidated upon meeting him for the first time, until he stuck out his hand and warmly welcomed me to Nicaragua. I knew immediately that I was standing before a true servant leader with a humble heart.

Bill's heart had been stolen by the children of Nicaragua. From the time he and his wife first visited the country in 1992 and witnessed how hard life is for families living in relentless poverty, their priorities changed. The couple abandoned their pursuit of successful careers and a comfortable lifestyle and set out to make a difference.

They discovered that 35 percent of the nation's children do not attend school. Of those that do, two-thirds fail to complete sixth grade. Bill decided he would start there, so he launched a non-governmental organization (NGO) to help Nicaragua educate its children.

He asked schools in the U.S. for donations and soon was receiving used desks and year-end surplus supplies of binders, glue, crayons, scissors, and partially used notebooks, things that Nicaraguan school children would otherwise do without. He purchased a warehouse to stockpile the material. Volunteers packed the items into shipping containers for transport to Nicaragua and distribution to a network of schools operating in impoverished neighborhoods.

Kids in impoverished neighborhoods lack many things besides education. Nutritious food is always in short supply. Bill's NGO did some research and found a source of packaged food consisting of a rice-soy casserole mixed with dehydrated vegetables and fortified with essential vitamins and minerals. Soon the shipping containers were sending tons of food packages to be served in school cafeterias so children from poor families could have at least one nourishing meal a day. Many of the churches in Bill's network also served the food at community soup kitchens.

Bill's NGO served Christian educators, as well. Each year, an advisory council that understood the needs of Nicaraguan teachers invited them to a two-day professional retreat, all expenses paid. In addition to refresher courses on educational issues, faculty members received classroom supplies and "teacher boxes" full of gift items specially selected for them.

The network of schools benefiting from the NGO's largess grew to 24 at the peak of its activity, serving thousands of children in communities across the country. From beginning to end, the vision to help schools educate Christian leaders for Nicaragua did not waver.

I write this account of Bill's work with a bit of melancholy. One, because this month marks seven years since his untimely death. Bill entered a U.S. hospital for routine gall bladder removal, agreeing to the procedure only when his doctor promised that he could return to Nicaragua on a short-term trip two weeks following the surgery. Unfortunately, three days after the operation, Bill took a sudden turn for the worse and passed away.

He was 69 years old.

A few days after his death, his wife told me in a phone call that she was worried about the NGO's future in Nicaragua. Over the previous year, the government had canceled the operating licenses of more than 1,100 private aid organizations serving the country. She asked that I not mention her name, nor the name of the NGO, for fear it might create trouble for their coworkers inside Nicaragua. This was the other reason for the melancholy.

Nevertheless, I am certain their legacy will outlast any setback that might arise. Bill's servant heart was a generous one and touched a lot of people. He relished passing on money and resources to organizations he

Southward Bound

thought were doing good work for the people of Nicaragua.

Among these was our international forum, which he evidently considered worthy of largesse. The conference he helped us organize in the pleasant retreat center in the coastal mountains attracted around 100 participants from seven countries. When it was over, Bill said he wanted to be sure that we balanced our budget. To my grateful surprise, he then handed me several thousand dollars to cover expenses.

There are heroes, and there are heroes. Some heroes become celebrities, household names. Their images, emblazoned on T-shirts and billboards, are universally recognized. Magazines, television shows and websites continually report their exploits to an admiring public.

We recognize some heroes by putting their names on streets, parks and schools, or depicting them in statues. It is a way of memorializing uncommon deeds done at a crucial moment in history.

But I suspect the majority of the world's true heroes are unsung. These are the men and women who leave earth a measurably better place than they found it, but whose names and legacies remain hidden to the rest of us.

That is, until Judgment Day. Then the scrolls will be unrolled, the sheep and goats separated, and we all will learn the names of those who fed the hungry, welcomed the stranger, clothed the naked and visited the prisoners.

Know anybody who might turn out to be that kind of hero?

I do.

----

*Dr. Daniel Villagra, pioneering physician, avid sportsman, and another genuine hero from Nicaragua.

Pura vida

There really is no other title you could put on a chapter about Costa Rica than *Pura Vida*. The phrase literally means "Pure Life" in English. *Ticos*, as the people of Costa Rica call themselves, use "pura vida" in everyday speech as a greeting or to express appreciation for something. Everyday life in this laid-back, user-friendly Central American country is best described as, well, pura vida.

Nicknamed the "Switzerland of Central America," Costa Rica staunchly defends human rights and diligently maintains political neutrality. Despite its small size, the country of five million has earned world-wide respect. Ticos are justifiably proud of their personal freedoms, stable economy, solid educational system and history of sensible solutions to political disputes.

Add to this scene of civic tranquility a lush, tropical landscape and pleasant temperatures year-round. The climate of the capital, San Jose, is described as "eternal springtime." With its fascinating flora and fauna, and two seashores that provide abundant sport fishing, diving and surfing, Costa Rica sounds like paradise on earth. Okay, maybe not quite. But pura vida, for sure.

Costa Rica attracts a lot of foreign visitors, a fact illustrated as we were crossing the border from Nicaragua in our aged Camry. There we encountered a tall, sandy haired man in black riding clothes who told us he had ridden his motorcycle down from Alaska and was headed for Patagonia and the extreme southern tip of South America.

A black-clad, bearded cyclist was also crossing the border at that moment, pointed in the opposite direction. The man was from Argentina and told us he had started his trip in Patagonia, headed for Alaska. I thought it a noteworthy coincidence that the two bikers were crossing paths at the exact midpoint of the 13,000-mile ride.

The first place we headed once we cleared immigration was the beach. We considered it our duty to Ben and Molly, who had by now spent an entire month cooped up with Mom and Dad in our aged Camry. They deserved the chance to kick back and enjoy sunshine, salt air and warm surf for a couple days.

Costa Rica has an endless supply of beaches. Bounded by a 185-mile stretch of the Caribbean along its northeastern shoreline, 630 miles of warm Pacific Ocean on the opposite coast and just a few hours of travel time between them, the country offers more sand and surf per square mile than any place I know.

This is an informed opinion, by the way. Barbara and I spent a year in the early 1980s living in San Jose while studying at the *Instituto de Lengua Española*, a language school that trains missionaries destined for service in Latin America. Because we were newlyweds with no children and no other professional duty than to learn Spanish, we made it our quest to enjoy as many beaches as one can in a year's time.

Many weekends found us on a bus headed to one or another coastal destination, from slow and steamy Puerto Viejo in the east to world-renown Manuel Antonio on the southwest coast. Of course, we made profitable advantage of the trips to learn Spanish, ahem.

Our favorite beach was Samara in Guanacaste Province, and that was where we headed with Ben and Molly. The first time Barbara and I had visited Samara, it was surrounded by cattle pastures whose fences nearly touched the sand. Thanks to Costa Rica's attraction to foreigners, luxury condominiums and gated communities border the sand nowadays. Yet, Samara manages to maintain its relaxing pace and laid-back charm.

You can still learn Spanish here, too. There are dozens of mom-and-pop language schools in town catering to foreigners. They will even put you up and feed you while you're at it. We're talking pura vida here.

Costa Rica was not always an enchanting place. In 1719, the colonial governor assigned to the region described it as "the poorest and most miserable Spanish colony in all America." His assessment was based largely on the absence of gold and silver, resources of primary interest to Europeans of the time.

The country did possess a rich natural resource that would

prove to be a gold mine in later years. The fertile soil on Costa Rica's well-watered mountainsides is some of the best in the world for growing coffee. First planted in 1808, it soon surpassed tobacco, sugar, and cacao as Costa Rica's primary export and remained its principal source of wealth well into the 20th century.

Ticos carry on a friendly rivalry with Colombians as to which of them produce the best beans. The competition has inspired a clever jest about Juan Valdez, the poncho-clad coffee farmer whose image, standing alongside his burro, has become Colombia's official icon for promoting its coffee as the world's best.

"Ah, but haven't you heard?" Ticos say with a wink. "Juan Valdez drinks coffee from Costa Rica."

Costa Ricans credit one man more than any other for their country's modern success. José María Hipólito Figueres Ferrer, known to his countrymen by his nickname "Pepe", could be called the nation's George Washington and Abraham Lincoln rolled into one.

Pepe Figueres was born into the family of a country doctor in 1906. At age 18 he left for Boston to study hydroelectric engineering at the Massachusetts Institute of Technology, returning four years later to become, you guessed it, a coffee farmer.

He turned his plantation into a laboratory for egalitarian practices. Figueres built substantial housing and recreational facilities for his workers, and provided them with medical care. A community garden and dairy supplied free vegetables and milk for plantation families.

Around the time of WWII, tensions between rival political parties threatened to destroy Costa Rican democracy. Figueres responded by training the Caribbean Legion, a militia force of 700. In 1948, he launched a revolution along with other landowners and student agitators. In the bitter, 44-day struggle, the rebels defeated a coalition of army troops and communist guerrillas to unseat the government.

This all-too-familiar scenario produced quite unprecedented results. The victors formed a provisional council over which Figueres presided. The council immediately abolished Costa Rica's standing army, granted voting rights to women and persons of color, and oversaw the drafting of a new constitution by a democratically elected assembly. Once the reforms were in place, council members resigned and yielded power to duly elected president, Otilio Ulate.

His countrymen, impressed by his bold action and impeccable integrity, elected Pepe Figueres president in 1953 and again in 1970. His tenure at the helm of government produced more democratic reforms and fostered steady prosperity. Ticos like to mention, with justifiable pride, that their country employs more teachers than policemen. The modest boast reveals something striking about the legacy of Pepe Figueres.

Figueres enhanced his legacy yet further by correcting a historic wrong. In the 1870s and '80s, Costa Rica brought thousands of Jamaicans to build a railroad from San José to the Caribbean port of Limón. Officials considered the immigrants, who were of African descent, better suited than native Ticos to work in the steamy jungles of the coast.

As often happens with immigrants, Jamaicans worked for lower wages than the locals. Many died from disease and accident. Unfortunately, their sacrifices did not earn them equivalent gratitude and respect. Afro-Caribbeans and their descendants could not reside outside the coastal province of Limón. Laws prohibited them from even traveling to the rest of the country and mingling with whites.

Pepe Figueres and his fellow revolutionaries ended this deplorable policy in 1949. They saw to it that Costa Rica's new constitution granted full rights of citizenship to all persons, despite their ethnicity.

Many of the Jamaican immigrants who built the railroad were evangelical Christians who planted scores of churches on the northeast coast and along the railroad line. One of their descendants, Pastor Irma, is a friend of ours.

She doesn't talk about it much, but Pastor Irma led a hard life before she found Jesus. Her demeanor is serious, almost stern, hinting at the abuse and violence she witnessed, or perhaps experienced, in her pre-Christian days. Irma comes across as a no-nonsense, street-smart lady who tolerates no fools.

But under that tough exterior beats a heart that loves people, particularly lost people who have yet to find God. Not content to win souls just in her downtown neighborhood, she has planted several more churches around the city of Limon. The congregations are populated with ex-drug addicts, former prostitutes, recovering alcoholics and people who, like Pastor Irma, led a hard life before meeting Jesus.

Once it fell to Barbara and me to organize a staff retreat in Costa Rica for missionaries serving in Latin America. We made sure that our schedule permitted us to worship on a Sunday morning in Pastor Irma's church. She greeted our group shyly, suggesting that one of us should preach that morning. She felt it was proper protocol to invite visiting missionaries into her pulpit.

"No way," I said, with a wink at my colleagues. "We are all on vacation today."

We had agreed beforehand to decline an invitation to preach, and it was absolutely the right call. As soon as Pastor Irma mounted the platform to help lead the lively hymns favored by persons of African descent, the serious demeanor fell away and she was caught up in enthusiastic, joy-of-the-Lord praise.

Pastor Irma preached that morning on the resurrection. She delivered a comprehensive, high-energy narration of Jesus' triumph over death, what it accomplished for His followers then, and what it promises for His followers today. It was a memorable meeting.

The meeting was about to become even more memorable. Near the end of the service, an usher called me to the back of the chapel to pray for a woman who had suddenly fallen unconscious. One of our missionary colleagues, a doctor, could not revive her and ordered that she be taken to the hospital. Sadly, she was dead on arrival.

We received this news over lunch with Pastor Irma and her congregation in the church basement.

Pura vida

The dead woman, a single mother of two in her late 30s, had suffered a massive heart attack. The tragedy left us understandably shocked and saddened.

None were more saddened than Pastor Irma. She explained to us that the young mother had used drugs and alcohol for much of her life. The abuse likely wore her heart down to the point that it simply stopped beating.

"She gave her life to Jesus just last year," Irma said. "I baptized her in January."

We all fell silent as we contemplated the scenario. A young woman leading a hard life of abuse and violence finds Jesus through Pastor Irma. As a result, that young woman was now walking the streets of gold.

"I want to compliment you on the moving sermon you preached this morning on the resurrection," I said to Pastor Irma. "This young woman's story, well it's just a remarkable case study in the resurrection."

"It is a tragedy, of course, that she left behind two young sons. But think of how much more tragic it would have been if she had not found Jesus."

Life, and death, happens to everybody. Sooner or later, every one of us must come to grips with dying. Jesus' words, quoted by Pastor Irma in her message that Sunday, puts the issue in very clear terms.

"I am the resurrection and the life; he who believes in me, though he die, yet shall he live, and whoever lives and believes in me shall never die" (John 11.25-26).

When you think about it, isn't this simply pura vida at its best?

The world's crossroad

Central America is lush and tropical. But as you drive south through this fascinating land bridge between North and South America, it seems to become even more lush and tropical. The vegetation gets thicker and the air more humid. Most of all, the rain falls harder and more often.

Panama lies at the southern end of Central America and gets a huge share of the sub-continent's rainfall. That is a good thing. You could even say that Panama is Panama because of its abundant rainfall. Okay, the rain and the fact that in the middle of the country the land bridge narrows down to a mere 50 miles between the Atlantic and Pacific Oceans.

That is where the Panama Canal is situated. Surely, if you have heard of Panama, you have heard of the Panama Canal, or maybe vice versa.

The Canal is famous for several reasons, but one in particular stands out to this writer. Unlike most waterways that link two oceans, the Panama Canal is full of fresh water. That is because it has to cross Central America's Continental Divide. It's tough enough for highways and railroads to cross continental divides. For a waterway that carries ocean-going vessels, it is infinitely tougher.

Crossing the Divide was the main reason why it cost tens of thousands of lives, decades of time

The world's crossroad

and zillions of dollars to build the Panama Canal. The project stymied the Spanish who first envisioned it, bankrupted the French who initiated it, and compelled the U.S.A. to deploy navy gunboats to finish it. When it was finally completed a little more than a hundred years ago, civil engineers ranked it as one of the seven wonders of the modern world.

The Canal's designers solved the Continental Divide problem by first digging a deep, wide passage known as the Culebra Cut through the mountains. This proved no small feat. Steam shovels took more than 20 years to excavate the Cut.

Meanwhile, engineers built a dam on the Chagres River to create Gatun Lake, the largest man-made lake in the world at the time. When it was complete, water from the huge reservoir flooded the Culebra Cut and, *voila*, the Panama Canal was born.

A series of locks raise ships 85 feet from sea level up to the surface of Gatun Lake. The trip across the lake itself accounts for a third of the 50-mile transit between oceans. Gatun Lake also supplies the water the canal needs to keep ships afloat.

It takes a lot of water to keep ships afloat in the Canal.

Panama's prodigious rainfall keeps Gatun Lake full of water. On average, 10 feet of rain falls every year on the Gatun Lake watershed. As much as 16 feet has been measured in some parts of the rainforest surrounding the lake. Scientists have determined that part of this precipitation is produced by the trees themselves, which trap atmospheric moisture and turn it into rain.

This codependency of trees, rain, canal, ships and money has turned Panamanians into some of the world's most ardent conservationists. They are passionate protectors of the rainforest. Anyone who cuts down a tree in the Gatun Lake watershed without a government permit will face astronomical fines and a possible prison term. Strict protection of the environment has preserved one of the world's most pristine biospheres around the Canal. Botanists and biologists come here from around the globe to research tropical plants and animals.

The Panama Canal has earned the country a national nickname: the World's Crossroad. This is no misnomer. Every year, more than 13 thousand ships transit the canal. Nearly one million have passed through the waterway since it first opened in 1914.

The 12-hour passage doesn't come cheap. Tolls start at $60,000 dollars but can reach three times that amount with added fees. Nevertheless, the Canal remains the preferred option to the long and sometimes treacherous voyage around South America's Cape Horn.

Anyone who goes to Panama should visit its famous canal. You can't miss it, really. The waterway skirts the city limits of the nation's capital and can be seen when taking off from or landing at the country's main airport.

If you drive from the U.S.A. to Panama as we did, your road trip ends at the Canal. A few miles beyond it, the southbound highway peters out in a dense no-man's land known as the Darien Gap. Nobody in their right mind ventures into The Gap.

So, this was the end of the road for our aged Camry, literally. By prior agreement, we gifted the car to fellow missionaries Mark and Janisse. Janisse's father, a part-time taxi driver, took us on a tour of the Canal, our farewell to the trusty Toyota and fitting closure to this segment of the Epic.

Should you ever visit the Canal, your tour guide might mention some little-known facts about this wonder of the modern world.

 > Construction of the Canal required the removal of 286 million cubic yards of dirt and rocks. That is roughly 25 times as much earth excavated to build the Channel Tunnel that today links the British Isles with continental Europe.
 > Ships actually transit the Isthmus of Panama from north to south, and vice versa. The Atlantic entrance to the Canal at Limon Bay lies east of

The world's crossroad

the waterway's mouth on the Pacific. Hence, this is the only place on the planet where the route from the Atlantic to the Pacific Ocean goes from west to east.

> In 1977, U.S. President Jimmy Carter and Panama's leader Omar Torrijos signed treaties that transferred ownership of the Canal to Panama. The agreement had been negotiated over the course of four U.S. administrations and, while criticized by some, proved immensely popular with Latin American republics. Some 20 heads of state were present at the signing ceremony in Washington, more than had ever attended an official event together in the history of the hemisphere.

The Canal has turned Panamá into the world's crossroad in several respects. The banks that handle the $3.5 billion dollars generated annually from its operation have turned Panama City into an important financial hub. Their gleaming skyscrapers give the urban skyline an appearance something like Hong Kong or lower Manhattan.

Panama's Tocumen International Airport has become an important hub for the world's airlines. Each year 16 million passengers traveling between North and South America, Europe and Asia pass through Tocumen.

It was at this airport several years ago that I first met Candido, the newly elected national leader of our church in Panama. I had an overnight layover and thought it a generous gesture to invite him to breakfast.

Whether he thought it generous of me or not, he never said. Accepting my invitation required him to make a two-hour trip across the Isthmus from his home near Colon in the wee hours of the morning. He arrived bleary eyed, sleepy and unshaven, but gracious.

A quiet, unassuming man with a solid physique hardened by his work as a bricklayer, Candido came up through the ranks to his leadership position in the church. He didn't tell me his story that day at breakfast. Barbara and I would learn about his unconventional career trajectory on a subsequent visit to his church in Cativá.

Not long after Candido and his wife found Jesus in the little church, the pastor announced that he was moving away and leaving Candido in charge of the congregation. Despite having no theological training and knowing next to nothing about how to pastor a church, Candido graciously accepted the assignment.

His decision was to cost him a share in a thriving business. He and his brother operated a shop across the street from the church. When Candido told his brother that he had become a pastor, the man stared at him in disbelief.

"Well, in that case, you are going to have to sell me your half of the business," he said.

"By why?" Candido asked, confused.

"Because, Brother, we are a liquor store. You cannot pastor a church and sell liquor at the same time. Don't you know that?"

Candido did not know that, so uninitiated was he to ecclesiastical matters. Nevertheless, he accepted the deal as part of God's plan.

Candido went to work in the building trades to support his family. He also set to work building up the congregation. It certainly needed building up. Following the former pastor's departure, exactly three members of the congregation remained: Candido's wife, his mother-in-law, and him.

Candido had never attended a clergy conference and so had no information about strategies to increase church attendance. Nor did he have any money or means to invest in ad campaigns or special events. The one thing he knew how to do was to pray. So Candido began to pray.

The world's crossroad

He rose every morning at five o'clock, went to the church chapel and sat in one of the empty pews. He prayed that God would bring a person to fill that seat in that pew. Then he moved over one place and prayed for God to bring someone else to fill that seat, and so on.

Within two years, the chapel was filling up every Sunday with eager worshippers. Candido had prayed his way through all the empty pews. He eventually baptized 110 new believers. His was one of the fastest growing congregations in Cativá.

Candido told Barbara and me this story as we sat in the chapel on a weekday morning. The only evidence of this robust growth to be seen was a missing wall. Candido had torn it out to add an extension to the building. With a bit of quiet pride, unusual for this unassuming man, he explained the reason.

"We began to notice that a lot of kids in our neighborhood didn't have enough to eat," he said. "So, we started cooking free meals for them."

"Word got around and now we have a lot of kids coming here to eat. We are building a dining hall to accommodate them.

"Of course, we tell them about Jesus, too," he added. "I have baptized some of them."

Whenever I think about Candido and his church, I end up with two impressions that are as unmistakable as they are personal. First, I am glad that he had no information on strategies to increase church attendance and thus was obliged to start with prayer. Sounds to me a lot like how Jesus started out building His church.

Second, I can now picture two wonders of the world in Panama. Its renowned, awe-inspiring Canal, and an unknown but awesome little church in Cativá.

Pearl of the Caribbean

Travelers have three options to get from Panama to Colombia. You can fly from Panama City, a brief, up-and-down hop. Or you can go by water on a private sailboat from Colón, which is not brief. The trip typically takes a month, allowing for stops on the San Blas islands for sunbathing and diving. Finally, you can travel by land through the Darien Gap.

Well really, there are only two options because sane people who love life never attempt to cross the Darien Gap. Its 60 miles of tortuous jungle and swamp is infested by deadly snakes, lethal insects, predatory animals, drug traffickers and guerillas. [Editor's note: we are not talking gorillas here, like you see in Tarzan movies, but guerrillas, as in armed outlaws that shoot travelers or kidnap them for ransom, or both.]

We once saw a documentary film about Arthur Blessitt, a man who in literal obedience to Jesus' command to take up his cross, trekked across every country of the world dragging a wooden cross that had once hung in his church in Hollywood.

The movie showed clips of Blessitt at different points in his 43,000-mile journey traversing barren deserts and frozen mountain ranges. He walked across big cities and active war zones. Once, in obedience to

Pearl of the Caribbean

Jesus, he crossed the No Man's Land between the Israeli army and the PLO to pray with Yasser Arafat. In short, Blessitt did some crazy stuff.

At one point in the documentary, the interviewer asks, "Arthur, in all your travels, when did you most fear for your life?"

Blessitt's expression darkens and he says, almost in a whisper, "Crossing the Darien Gap. I was sure that I was going to die there."

Our policy on the Epic was to avoid death whenever possible. And a month on the water offered little appeal for one prone to debilitating seasickness as I am. So, to get to Colombia we opted for the short flight from Panama City. It took us to Cartagena, the Pearl of the Caribbean.

Nearly 500 years old, Cartagena is a treasure for several reasons. Strategically located on the north coast of South America, it became imperial Spain's preferred port for shipping silver mined in the Andes Mountains to Europe. The trade generated enormous wealth for Cartagena's citizens, who built charming colonial homes, ornate churches and stately public buildings that grace the city center to this day.

The wealth, in turn, made Cartagena a primary target of pirates and British warships. Cartagena endured frequent sieges and naval bombardments by enemies intent on capturing The Pearl.

A visit to Cartagena should include some hours spent at San Felipe de Barajas, a massive stone fortress with a commanding view of the harbor and a labyrinth of underground tunnels. It stands as a monument to the centuries of assault and resistance.

The toughest challenge came in 1741, when an armada of 180 ships and 25,600 men under the command of Admiral Edward Vernon laid siege to Cartagena during one of several wars between Britain and Spain. Despite his formidable force, Vernon's assault on San Felipe de Barajas failed, leaving 800 British dead and another 1,000 taken prisoner. The defeated admiral lifted the siege and withdrew, thus ending what proved to be the last attempt by a foreign power to conquer The Pearl.

The battle produced an interesting historical footnote. Vernon had recruited 2,000 infantrymen from England's North American colonies for the campaign. Among them was a young man named Lawrence Washington. When he returned home from the war, Washington named his Virginia plantation in honor of his commanding officer. Mount Vernon, later the home of Lawrence's famous half-brother George, thus became a kind of testament to the battle for Cartagena.

For myself, I consider Cartagena a pearl because as well as being a place of charming beauty and fascination, it is the historic gateway to one of the finest countries in the world. Rather than expound on the many charms of Colombia to describe its allure, or try to explain its perplexing paradox, I will share this fanciful legend that Colombians invented about their homeland.

In the days of creation, God announced to the angels that He was going to create a very special country. "This is how it will be," He said. "Two oceans, the balmy Caribbean and the mighty Pacific, will bathe its shores. The heavens will provide warm winds and abundant rainfall, so that it will never know ice or snow or drought. I shall fashion a great, tropical plain in the east, where immense herds of cattle will graze. In the west, broad rivers will flow between verdant mountain ranges. Rich soils shall produce all manner of good food, as well as the world's finest coffee. The forests will shelter myriad species of animals and exotic birds. Under the ground I shall sow petroleum, precious metals and emeralds. The name of this special country shall be called 'Colombia.'"

The astonished angels gasped. "Lord, such a land will truly be a paradise. But what of the countries round about? When they see how you favored Colombia, they will be jealous and say that you were not fair to endow it with such riches."

Pearl of the Caribbean

"I shall be fair," God replied, "because I shall populate this special country with...Colombians."

My Colombians friends will share this tongue-in-cheek story about themselves when discussing their nation's penchant for violence. During the past century, Colombia developed a reputation as one of the world's most dangerous countries. In the 1980s and '90s, it suffered the highest homicide rate in the Americas, 15 times that of the United States. The country was home to the planet's most ruthless drug cartels and outlaw militia armies.

Theories abound to explain why this was, but none are ultimately convincing because Colombians are a truly amiable people. Among Latin Americans known for warm and gracious manners, Colombians are the warmest and most gracious.

A friend whose husband was posted to Venezuela with the British Foreign Office spent several holidays in Cartagena and fell in love with Colombia. She once told me, "I really don't think I would mind if a Colombian shot me dead because he would be so nice about it."

Certainly, history has played a part in creating the violence. In 1948, an assassin shot dead the popular politician Jorge Gaitán in broad daylight on a busy Bogotá street. The callous murder sparked a bloody struggle between the country's two principal political parties. *La Violencia*, as this dark chapter in Colombia's history came to be known, claimed an estimated 200,000 lives. Most died at the hands of partisan militias who roved the countryside at will, robbing and killing innocent civilians.

Politicians finally compromised and La Violencia subsided in the 1960s, but not before spawning the formation of left-leaning guerrilla armies such as the Revolutionary Armed Forces of Colombia (FARC) and the National Liberation Army (ELN). Together they carried on the longest running insurrection (52 years) in Latin American history.

Conflict can produce great men and women. Colombia has had its share of both. After two days in Cartagena, we carried on to the town of Sincelejo to visit one of them. Our son Ben refers to him as the Gandhi of Colombia.

Ricardo Esquivia was born and raised during La Violencia. When he was nine years old, his father entered a leprosarium. Ricardo enrolled in a nearby boarding school operated by Mennonite missionaries.

At age 13, Ricardo confessed faith in Christ and was baptized. By the time he entered high school, he had developed a clear idea about his life's work. He was to fight against violence and unjust circumstances. He believed he could best fulfill that calling by becoming a lawyer.

In 1983 he left a lucrative law practice in Bogotá and moved his young family north to the Caribbean coast. His reason: to help change the circumstances of poorly paid and excessively exploited farm workers.

Esquivia's work was exhausting and dangerous. Once, police arrested one of his clients, the leader of a farmers union in San Jacinto. Two days later the man's body was found riddled with nearly 50 bullets. He left behind a wife and four children.

Ricardo's work turned yet more dangerous when ELN rebels began infiltrating the farmers unions. One night 60 soldiers broke into the Esquivia home and arrested Ricardo. Although he was released unharmed, he knew it was just a matter of time before his bullet riddled body would be found somewhere. He moved his family back to Bogotá.

I first met Ricardo in 1990 when he was working to introduce an article to Colombia's new constitution that would allow for alternative service to the country's compulsory military draft. He saw the measure as step toward reducing the cycle of violence that plagued Colombia.

"The military teaches young men to kill," he explained to me. "When they leave the army, some join the rebel groups or right-wing paramilitaries. Others accept lucrative jobs with the drug cartels."

"We believe that if we can offer young men an alternative to this lifestyle, it will help to break Colombia's cycle of violence."

When we caught up with Ricardo Esquivia in Sincelejo years later, he was again living on the north coast, working to break Colombia's cycle of violence. We were privileged to witness him in action, changing the result of unjust circumstances.

The case involved about two dozen farm families. One day right-wing paramilitaries invaded their small isolated community and forced everybody to gather in the village plaza.

"We know you are rebel sympathizers," the militiamen falsely claimed. Then they chose two men from the crowd and shot them dead.

"The rest of you have 24 hours to clear out, or the same thing will happen to you," they declared before leaving.

The stunned villagers buried the dead men and left as ordered. The paramilitaries later returned to burn down their houses and confiscate their livestock and crops.

Ricardo had arranged a day-long seminar with the displaced farmers. We listened in rapt attention as they expressed their anger at the injustice, reckoned their losses and discussed what they were going to do.

Ricardo patiently led them through the alternatives. One, they could buy guns and go after the culprits. No, they decided after some discussion, that would only bring more death. The cycle of violence would go on like a revolving door.

Two, they could bring a court case to bring the culprits to justice and regain their land. This would be a risky venture, with no guarantee of a satisfactory result. It was common knowledge that militia groups operated with the tacit support of wealthy businessmen and politicians in Bogotá.

Three, they could plant yams. Ricardo told them about "Sowing Peace," a project to help victims of these attacks recover economically. Sowing Peace would provide them a plot of land and seed. Once the crop was ready, wholesalers would buy their yams for export to Africa.

By this time, it was late in the afternoon. The tense and combative atmosphere of the morning had settled into a reasoned acceptance of non-violent options. The families voted to plant yams.

Reflecting on this incident, it occurred to me that it had taken place quite close to Cartagena, practically in The Pearl's backyard. Tourists who come to admire San Felipe de Barajas, the fortress so formidable in repelling foreign enemies, could scarcely imagine the desperate struggles occurring a few miles inland. Talk about a paradox.

The good news today is that violence is trending downward in Colombia. The country's homicide rate has plummeted since the 1990s. Peace treaties have been signed with guerrilla armies. Travelers no longer risk being kidnapped or shot when traveling the countryside. International tourists are once again discovering the beauty and fascination of Colombia.

I reckon that one reason Colombia is enjoying greater peace is because Ricardo Esquivia answered God's call in high school. Perhaps his seminar that day in Sincelejo was but a minor victory in the battle to break the cycle of violence. Nonetheless, minor victories persistently won by faithful men and women can eventually change circumstances.

Medellin

The first time I stepped off the plane at Medellin's International Airport, the sensation was something like what Dorothy must have felt when she stepped off the porch of her plain Kansas farmhouse into the Land of Oz. The place was literally magical, with greener grass, sweeter air and silence mountains more majestic than any I had ever seen.

The airport sits on a plateau two thousand feet above Medellin and the road winds down steep mountainsides to the city center at the bottom of the Aburrá Valley. I sat silent in the back seat of the taxi for three quarters of an hour, awed by the stunning scenery.

Just as we were entering the city limits, I noticed a large patch of scorched earth on the side of the road. The cab driver must have read my thoughts because he remarked, "Oh yeah, the FARC burned a bus there this morning."

I immediately pictured what must have happened. This was the early 1990s, when the war dragged on between Colombia and the Revolutionary Armed Forces of Colombia, the FARC. To bankroll their rebellion, urban terrorists set up roadblocks to hijack city busses. They then forced passengers off the bus at gunpoint and relieved them of all their money and valuables.

The FARC checked ID's and, if they discovered policemen or soldiers among the passengers, they shot them dead in full view of fellow commuters. If they discovered foreigners or journalists, they abducted them to be held for ransom.

Then before fleeing, the guerrillas set fire to the bus.

My mood suddenly changed from idyllic reverie to fear and trembling. You see, I was both a foreigner and a journalist. I had come to Medellin on my U.S. passport in order to interview Dr. Jaime Ortiz, the president of the Biblical Seminary of Colombia.

An attorney by training and influential delegate to Colombia's 1991 constitutional assembly, Ortiz had helped reshape the religious rights landscape in the country. I had an appointment to talk to him about it and write a story for a California-based new agency. Getting kidnapped had not entered into my calculations.

"How often do these bus burnings happen?" I asked the driver uneasily.

"Every couple of weeks or so," he said.

He looked in the rearview mirror and noticed my pale expression.

"You should be okay," he offered. "Just take taxis wherever you go."

I took his advice and survived to catch my flight out that afternoon, after a most interesting and productive interview with Dr. Ortiz.

Years later on the Epic journey, Barbara, Ben, Molly and I arrived in Medellin early one morning on an overnight bus. A hijacking or kidnapping had not once entered my mind when I purchased the tickets. Looking back, I realize this simple

Medellin

act was a sort of testament to the profound change Colombia had undergone since that first visit.

It was a gray, rainy morning and clouds obscured the majestic mountainsides as we made the steep descent into the city. Despite the disappointing weather, it was good to be back in Medellin.

I had made a half dozen trips to Medellin in the intervening years, yet the place never fails to fascinate. During our three days in town, Molly took her first hang gliding flight to celebrate her 23rd birthday. The pilot made a crash landing on a steep mountainside when wind currents abruptly shifted, but she survived to tell the tale.

Barbara and I saw the same aerial view of the Aburrá Valley from a gondola that is part of the city's public transportation system. Medellin was the first metropolitan center in the world to integrate cable lifts into its mass transit service. Six gondola lines carry commuters from train stations on the valley floor to lofty neighborhoods perched on the mountainsides above, and one ticket pays for the whole trip. The novel arrangement has earned Medellin a rank among the world's most innovative cities.

Innovation carries over into the art scene. Medellin has dedicated an entire plaza to display the sculpture of a famous son of the city, Fernando Botero. It requires an entire city plaza to accommodate Botero's oversized/overweight statues. His work is unforgettable, even for a lukewarm art lover like me.

At Ben's urging, we visited what is undoubtedly the most unforgettable of Botero's artwork. Our son later wrote this account in his journal.

"In a central plaza in the heart of Medellin stand a pair of monuments that reflect the Colombian paradox: two large bird sculptures that their creator named *Pajaros de la Paz* (Birds of Peace). They illustrate a nation at war with itself and yet bursting with energy and opportunity.

"Originally only a single bird, the first sculpture sustained massive damage when a bomb went off at its base and sent fatal shrapnel everywhere. Below the remains of the flightless fowl is a sobering list of bystanders who became another statistic that terrible day in a complicated web of violence."

The bombing happened in 1995, when Medellin was ranked as the most dangerous city in the world. The death toll was staggering, an average of 20 murders per day. Medellin's homicide rate in the 1990s was five to six times higher than the most violent cities in the U.S.

Much of the violence was perpetrated by drug cartels or urban guerrilla cells, but not all. Military intelligence identified 120 criminal gangs operating there. Specializing in homicide, kidnap and extortion, the gangs employed 3,000 *sicarios* (professional killers). That was one hitman for every 1,000 residents.

Politicians would sometimes hire sicarios to kill opponents. Businessmen hired them to settle scores when a deal went sour. Husbands hired them to eliminate unwanted wives.

The average Medellin sicario was 16 years of age, came from a dysfunctional family and saw little chance of finishing an education or landing a decent job. He, or she, saw murder-for-money as a way to escape the slum.

But few ever did. Low wages and fierce competition drove down the price for contracts. Sicarios would accept as little as $30 dollars to take a life.

Because of the fierce competition, sicarios mostly took each other's lives, which accounted for the vast majority of homicides in Medellin. The average life expectancy of a teenager who became a sicario was six months.

That was Medellin then. It is not Medellin today. The most dangerous city in the world reduced its homicide rate by 95% in the span of a dozen years. Murder and mayhem have disappeared from all but the city's toughest neighborhoods. Today you are as safe in Medellin as you would be in Columbus, Ohio.

What brought about the change?

Some say pacification started with the death in 1993 of the ruthless Medellin Cartel boss Pablo Escobar and the ensuing collapse of the Colombian drug trade. Others credit former President Álvaro Uribe and his 2002 "Operation Orion" that disarmed urban guerrilla groups and right-wing militias. Locals believe a string of innovative mayors who worked to integrate poor hillside neighborhoods with the more affluent city center, a process that reduced extreme poverty by 66 percent, did the most to transform the city.

No doubt these developments have had a major impact. But personally, I believe the transformation of Medellin began before these events, and in the most unlikely of places.

Bellavista National Jail, a prison on the outskirts of the city, used to be a much more dangerous place than Medellin itself. Built to house 1,500 inmates, by 1990 Bellavista teemed with nearly 5,000 drug dealers, sicarios and terrorists. It had become a microcosm of Medellin's death culture, concentrated and intensified.

Inside its walls, practiced killers murdered one another with terrifying regularity for money, revenge or simple amusement. On average, 20 inmates and corrections officers died each month inside Bellavista. A visiting criminologist pronounced it the deadliest prison in the Western world.

The death toll skyrocketed when prison guards went on strike and riots broke out. Unsupervised inmates attacked each other in bloody hand to hand combat. Corpses littered the corridors of Bellavista. Killers cut off arms and legs, gouged out eyes and used their victims' blood to write obscene graffiti on the walls.

Medellin's press corps gathered every day at the gates of Bellavista to report the latest body count. One day it was 8, the next 13, then 22 and so on. Prison staff urged the warden to call in the army to quell the rioting.

Instead, the warden accepted a suggestion from the prison's chaplain Oscar Osorio to organize an evangelistic campaign. Christian inmates and civilian volunteers formed prayer bands to intercede for the prison. They marched through the corridors singing hymns and praying for the inmates. At one point, they gave each one a tiny white flag and told them, "When you hear the national anthem playing on the loudspeakers, raise your flag, bow your head and pray with us."

It was undoubtedly the most unorthodox tactic to quell a prison riot ever devised, but it worked. When the anthem played, the prayers went up and the killing stopped. An eyewitness described the scene.

"Many were converted in the campaign. The deaths started dwindling until there was not one single casualty. Many surrendered their blades and pistols. One day, a whole group of prisoners handed over their weapons to Chaplain Osorio himself."

"People were saying, 'Something strange has happened here. We feel something like peace and joy. Even though I don't believe in God, what He does is real.'"

Medellin's press corps grew skeptical when, for several consecutive days, the guards reported zero body counts. The reporters suspected the army of staging a night-time strike that had ended in a massacre. They insisted that the warden allow them entry to the prison, where they expected to find mass graves and the stench of death.

Instead, they saw crowds of prisoners in their cell blocks singing hymns, praying fervently and studying the Bible. When the reporters asked the inmates what had happened, one replied, "Bellavista has a new boss, the Lord Jesus Christ. He has taken over this jail."

If they did not accept this explanation, the press corps had to accept the facts. Bellavista had been suddenly, radically transformed. The zero body-count continued. In fact, six years would pass without a single inmate dying violently inside the prison walls.

Authorities of Colombia's penal system took note of what was going on in Bellavista and wondered if it might be replicated in other jails. When they learned that professors and students from the

Biblical Seminary of Colombia were operating a training institute for inmates, they approached them with a proposal. If Bible professors would recommend graduates who showed promise, the authorities would transfer them in teams of two to other prisons to do missionary work.

Bellavista inmates volunteered for the program and within a few years, prison missionaries were at work in Ibague, Cali, Palmira, Calarcá, Tolima and Barranquilla. Transformations similar to Bellavista's began happening in those jails.

Transformations began happening on the streets of Medellin, as well. During a 2004 visit to Medellin, a professor at the Biblical Seminary of Colombia introduced me to members of a gang who had elected to renounce violence. When attacked by a rival gang, they refused to retaliate, even when one of their own was killed.

The gang disposed of its weapons, installed computers at their headquarters and began teaching neighborhood kids useful skills to help them finish their education. Their stand for non-violence eventually convinced other gangs to follow suit and stop killing each other.

Medellin today is not quite the Land of Oz, but its transformation from the world's most dangerous city to one that ranks high on the quality-of-life index is truly miraculous.

And for that, I think, we have to give at least some credit to the Prince of Peace.

The Bolivarians

I would strongly discourage anyone from attempting a family road trip across Venezuela. Given the country's severe shortages of food, fuel, water and electricity, and the high incidence of robbery, carjacking, kidnap and murder, your chances of finishing the trip are pretty much zero.

Our family nearly failed to make the crossing on the Epic journey, and that was before Venezuela's dictators had completely destroyed the economy, demolished infrastructure and erased the rule of law. In our case, the near failure was due to a severe shortage of judgment on the part of our tour leader (that would be me). I fell prey to an old-fashioned shakedown.

We walked into the scam minutes after crossing the border from Cucuta, Colombia, on the Francisco de Paula Santander International Bridge. Friends had advised us to take a taxi from the border to the next major bus station, 31 miles away in San Cristobal. This would save us time, they said.

Time was of the essence because we hoped to catch the overnight express bus that left San Cristobal at 5:00 in the afternoon. We might have made it, had we not taken the taxi we did. The driver prolonged the normal one and a-half hour transit (yes, that works out to 20 miles per hour) so that just as we pulled into

San Cristobal, we witnessed the 5:00 o'clock bus express exiting the station.

No worries, the cab driver told us. He had friends who could get us tickets on the next overnight bus, and introduced us to two friendly individuals. They said tickets were sold out but they could pull some strings for us, which they evidently did.

"You can't board at the station itself," they announced later, when handing over the tickets. "But no worries, the bus will stop for you at the edge of town."

The same obliging cab driver dropped us off at the appointed spot and we boarded the bus in gathering gloom. Barbara and I settled into our seats on the lower level. Ben, Molly and Lindsey, a high school friend of Molly's who had joined us in Bogotá, climbed the stairway to the upper deck and took their seats. All was well, or so we thought.

About 15 miles outside of town the bus pulled to the side of the road and the driver came back to tell Barbara and me that our party had to get off the bus. "I have to pick up other passengers ahead," he explained," and I need your seats. It is impossible for you to stay on this bus."

"You can't be serious!" I retorted. But he was.

"Well then, give us back our money," I said, feeling the blood drain from my face. Realizing that we were now in total darkness in a deserted stretch of jungle, I added, "And call us a taxi to take us back to town."

"I can't do that," he said. "I only have half the money. You will have to find the guy who sold you the tickets to get the other half."

And no, he could not arrange for a taxi to pick us up.

"Señor," I said, now feeling the blood rushing back to my face, which turned bright crimson, "there is no way we are getting off this bus unless we get a full refund and a taxi back to town."

The driver turned on his heel and went back to the front of the bus, I assumed to get reinforcements. We gathered Ben, Molly and Lindsey and told them what was happening. I can't remember if my voice was trembling, but I was.

"Dad, let's pray," Ben said at once. It sounded like a good idea, better than any that our tour leader could come up with.

So, we huddled at the bottom of the bus's stairway and prayed. I confess that it was one of the sincerest prayers I have ever uttered in my life.

No sooner had we pronounced "Amen" than a stranger appeared on the stairway.

"Is this driver trying to throw you off the bus?" he asked.

"Well, yes he is," we said.

"This is outrageous!" the man said. "They do this all the time to foreigners. We are not going to let it happen."

About then the driver reappeared with the conductor and the stranger got in his face. I can't remember what he said, but it startled the driver.

The rest of the passengers in our compartment overheard the man and joined in.

"You are a disgrace!" they yelled at the driver. "Let these poor people alone, or else we are going to throw *you* off the bus!"

This outburst completely unhinged the driver. He turned on his heel and retreated to his compartment. The passengers broke into boisterous cheers and applause.

The noise died down and I mustered the composure to thank our fellow travelers for their support. They waved and smiled and said that it was all good. We settled back into our seats and the bus started moving. After a while, the lights went out and we fell asleep.

We awoke in early daylight as the bus neared Caracas, the country's capital. I said good morning to our fellow passengers and we struck up a conversation. When I asked where they were headed, they suddenly turned solemn and glanced at each other.

"Well, it's like this," a woman said quietly. "We are shopkeepers in the Cucutá city market. Until last week, that is. A fire broke out in the market one night and entirely destroyed our shops, along with all our merchandise and money."

"We got together and pooled our money to buy tickets to Caracas in order to apply for government assistance. We hope they will help us with a loan so that we can start over."

I was shocked. Here were people who had lost their livelihood and, in some cases, their entire life savings. Yet they remained cheerful, friendly and fun-loving. Perhaps last night's rout of the corrupt bus driver had helped to ease their distress. I hope so. It had surely eased mine.

Their unselfish support and upbeat attitude left me with a high opinion of ordinary Venezuelans. Despite heartbreaking disaster, they still manage to be kind, generous and daring.

At this writing, heartbreaking disaster afflicts millions of Venezuelans. Almost everyone in the country has lost a career, a home and a future. Poverty, malnutrition and disease are unchecked in a country that was once one of the wealthiest in South America. The crime rate is the highest in the Western Hemisphere, with one murder committed every 21 minutes and 50 persons kidnapped every day. One in five of these crimes is reportedly committed by police officers or members of the military.

The onset of Venezuela's disaster began in 1998, when voters elected former army colonel Hugo Chavez to the presidency. A strident critic of traditional politicians and self-proclaimed champion of the common man, Chavez launched what he called the "Bolivarian Revolution," named for the country's founder, Simon Bolivar.

Bolivar was himself a revolutionary, one of history's most renowned, in fact. Orphaned at age nine and educated in Europe, he enlisted in the War of Independence against Spain in 1810. His military skill and shrewd ability to forge strategic alliances elevated Bolivar to Supreme Commander of the revolutionary army. By the end of the 15-year conflict, Bolivar had succeeded in liberating the territory that today encompasses the nations

The Bolivarians

of Venezuela, Colombia, Ecuador, Peru and Bolivia.

Those five countries were originally one. The vision of the Great Liberator, as he had come to be known, was a united republic stretching from the Caribbean coast to the southern Cone of South America. It would have been the largest and wealthiest nation on the continent had Bolivar's vision been realized.

However, Bolivia and Peru soon voted to go their separate ways. Despite the defections, Bolivar doggedly pursued the dream of a "Gran Colombia", narrowly escaping assassination for his trouble. Disillusioned with politics, he resigned his presidency in 1830 and died the same year of tuberculosis. Bolivar was 47.

Hugo Chavez appropriated Bolivar's name and fame for his political movement. He promised his countrymen a revolution that would carry Venezuela to a glorious future, following in the footsteps of the Liberator himself. But just as Bolivar failed to fulfill his vision, Chavez also failed. In fact, his revolution has ruined Bolivar's homeland to an extent that no one could have imagined.

Chavez funded his revolution with profits from Venezuela's huge petroleum industry. The country owns the largest proven oil reserves in the world, so Chavez had a lot of money to spend, especially because oil prices were at record levels in the first years of his presidency.

He created the Bolivarian Mission, a social program to provide health care and sports training to poor communities. The Mission constructed thousands of medical clinics and staffed them with doctors imported from Cuba.

But like so many of Chavez's promises, this one went unfulfilled. In 2007, the Venezuelan Medical Federation discovered that 70 percent of the Bolivarian clinics were either unfinished or abandoned.

If Chavez seemed unable to deliver on his promises, he was even more inept at stewarding the country's immense wealth. In 2003, he quashed an oil worker's strike by firing 18 thousand veteran employees of *Petroleos de Venezuela*, the massive state-owned company that generated one-quarter of GDP. He replaced them with his loyal followers, most of whom knew nothing about operating oil refineries, pumping stations or pipelines.

Oil production steadily declined, along with GDP, as poorly maintained plants failed and infrastructure decayed. When oil prices fell sharply between 2014 and 2016, the already battered national economy fell off a cliff. The bolivar, Venezuela's national currency, became worthless. World-record hyperinflation reduced wages to pennies a day, even for highly skilled professionals. Three out of four Venezuelans fell into extreme poverty. The average citizen lost 19 pounds because of food scarcity.

Nicolas Maduro, who occupied the presidency when Chavez died of cancer in 2013, declared an "economic emergency." To resolve the crisis, he suspended the National Assembly (Venezuela's Congress) and replaced the entire Supreme Court with persons of his choosing. In other words, Maduro turned what was left of the government into a full-blown dictatorship.

The repressive move obviously did not solve the problem. On the contrary, Maduro's measures plunged the country into complete chaos and misery. The exodus of economic refugees swelled to from 1.5 to 6 million. At this writing, one in five Venezuelans live in foreign countries.

But what of the other four in five? Well, as you probably have figured out by now, they must be determined and resourceful folks who can face heartbreaking disaster and still keep going.

Our cross-country bus trip ended in eastern Venezuela where two of my friends named Zabdiel live. They are the only two Zabdiels I know in the world and they both go by the nickname "Zabdy." Here I will call them Zabdy One and Zabdy Two.

Our first stop was the home of Zabdy One, a cozy, two-story house that could accommodate all five of us. The three days of warm hospitality we enjoyed there was a welcome break from cross-country bus travel, for sure.

Zabdy One spent his entire career working as a technician in the oil industry, but was fired when Petroleos de Venezuela went on strike in 2003. Only two years away from retirement, he lost his entire pension and benefits. He scrambled to support the family with occasional jobs in construction or machinery repair. Despite the unfair hardship he endured, he maintains an upbeat disposition, always ready with a joke, a warm handshake or an idea for some fun.

Zabdy One has a heart for God and the indigenous tribal peoples of Venezuela. When the occasional job earns him a bit of extra cash, he spends it on a four-hour trip to tribal settlements to preach and teach Bible. I had a couple opportunities over the years to go with him on these trips, and always noticed another new church that had sprung between my visits.

With our travel funds, we bankrolled a trip to the tribal communities so that Zabdy One could visit his friends and then drop us off at the home of Zabdy Two. The trip to the settlements took us past wide, empty pastures where immense herds of cattle once grazed. That was before Hugo Chavez expropriated the ranches because their owners opposed his politics and turned over management to his friends in the army. The generals soon annihilated the herds, slaughtering some to feed their troops and selling off the rest to line their pockets. The empty pastures are merely one illustration of why Venezuela suffers acute food shortages these days.

Zabdy Two is the son of Venezuelan missionaries to indigenous tribal peoples. He literally grew up on the rivers of eastern Venezuela, traveling with his parents in motorboats and dugout canoes to spread the gospel. He later earned an engineering degree in the U.S. and became a specialist in oil spill cleanup. After traveling the world for petroleum companies, he returned to Venezuela with a sizable chunk of change to invest in making his homeland a better place.

The idea Zabdy Two had for doing this connected his love of the jungle with broad experience in environmental repair. Christian ecologists call it Creation Care.

He discovered that turtles were fast becoming extinct in the rivers of eastern Venezuela, largely because tribal hunters were selling turtle eggs for cash to feed their families. He researched the price of turtle eggs and began offering the hunters a bit more than market price for their eggs. He soon cornered the turtle egg market.

Zabdy Two incubated the eggs and raised the hatchlings in large cement tanks. Once they reached appropriate size--about four inches in diameter-- he released the young turtles to the wild, several thousand at a time.

In addition to repopulating the rivers of eastern Venezuela with tiny turtles, Zabdy Two also hosted visitors in his rustic riverside resort. During our stay there, we enjoyed savory meals of fish and fried plantains, long hours snoozing in hammocks and fishing for piranha.

Before Venezuela became too dangerous for tourists, Zabdy Two hosted teams of international volunteers who traveled the rivers with him to share the gospel with tribal communities and deliver medical and dental care.

At this writing, no one can predict the future of Venezuela. Most Venezuelans, indeed most of the world, fervently hope that a competent and democratic government will replace the present dictatorship and create conditions for economic recovery and a return to the prosperous and pleasant country that Venezuela once was.

But if that is to happen, it will require measures profoundly more effective than those that have been attempted up until now. Opposition politicians have tried numerous times to unseat, first Chavez, and now Maduro, but to no avail. International pressure such as economic sanctions, harsh condemnation of the regime and threats of military intervention, has changed nothing. Venezuela's own security forces, packed with Maduro's military cronies and corrupt policemen, certainly have no interest in bringing down the dictatorship.

So that leaves the liberation of Venezuela squarely in the hands of its ordinary citizens. Determined and resourceful people who refuse to surrender to fear and despair are key to overcoming the country's evils. These are the Venezuelans who, like the two Zabdys and those lovely folks on our overnight bus, endure heartbreaking disaster every day, but still have the faith to be kind, generous and daring.

Amazonia

There are three places in South America that are definitely worth seeing and I suggest you do it sooner than later. I'm afraid humanity's bad habits may soon render them unrecognizable.

I'm talking about the Atacama Desert, Patagonia and the Amazon.

Well, actually, you don't have to rush to see the Atacama before it changes. Like the Sahara, vast stretches of its barren sands are uninhabitable. Human enterprise is not likely to ruin the Atacama because there is hardly anything there to ruin.

Come to think of it, Patagonia is probably safe for a couple more generations. Because it lies far from the rich countries of Asia, Europe and North America, relatively few of the world's international tourists visit its majestic mountain ranges and crystalline lakes each year.

Amazonia

About 90 percent of Patagonia is flat, arid sagebrush. The land can scarcely support the wandering herds of guanaco (a wild cousin of the llama) and Andean ostriches that call it home. A desperate change in the world economy would have to happen before industrialization and urban sprawl take root there.

Amazonia, on the other hand, is changing fast, very fast. Too fast for comfort, really. We are talking about a complex tropical ecosystem that harbors an astonishing variety of trees, birds, animals, fish and insects. The Amazon River Basin covers one-third of South America, roughly equal in size to the continental United States. Yet in a mere 50 years, nearly one-fifth of its jungles have been cleared and its human population has increased fourfold. Despite the fervent efforts of native tribal peoples and environmentalists, the pace of these changes is not likely to slow. You best get there as soon as you can.

The most memorable way to see the Amazon is from the deck of a riverboat. That's how we wanted to see it on the Epic, so we took an overnight bus from the Venezuela border to Manaus, the largest, busiest, steamiest city in the Brazilian state of Amazonas. [Editor's note: If somebody asks, you should know that Manaus is actually on the Rio Negro, a few miles upstream from where this river meets the Amazon. But don't worry, nobody ever asks.]

You should also know that, unless you want to take an airplane, riverboats are the only viable option to travel from Manaus to your next destination. Roads have yet to be built along the river, partly because of annual floods, mostly because traffic flows best on the Amazon itself (pun intended). Ocean-going ships can dock at Manaus, over 900 miles inland from the Atlantic. Vessels as large as 9,000 tons can continue upriver another 1,300 miles to Iquitos, Peru. Small wonder the Amazon River is one of South America's busiest freeways.

Did I say "small?" That's a word rarely used in a sentence about the Amazon. It is not the longest river in the world--the Nile barely edges it out in that category--but dwarfs contenders in every other category. The size of the Amazon is hard to fathom (another pun intended), but here are a few facts that might help put it into perspective.

- The Amazon contains more water than any other river on the planet, equal in volume to the next seven largest rivers combined.
- One-fifth of all the fresh water flowing into the world's oceans comes from the Amazon.

< Two of its tributary rivers are larger than the Mississippi.
< The distance from its source, a snow-fed stream in the Peruvian Andes, to its mouth at the Atlantic Ocean equals the distance from New York to Rome.
< At its widest points, the opposite shore cannot be seen by the naked eye.
< No bridge has ever been built across the Amazon.

When we got off the bus at the boat dock in Manaus, the first thing we did was to help Lindsey buy a hammock for our voyage. [Travel tip: Wait until the Manaus boat dock to buy a hammock. They come in all shapes and sizes and you are sure to find one that fits your particular contours. Also, they come with just the right length of rope to tether your hammock to the railings on the boat's sleeping deck. I had bought a cheap, lightweight hammock weeks before at an outdoor market in Nicaragua and envied Lindsey's choice.]

We enjoyed getting acquainted with Lindsey, whom Barbara and I first met when she joined the Epic in Bogotá. Sweet, patient, adaptable to heat, bugs and schedule changes, Lindsey made the best of traveling companions. I'm proud to say that, at this writing, we are still friends.

With hammocks and backpacks in tow, we took a skiff out to board our riverboat, which like every other vessel in its class was triple-decked, open-sided and painted white. [Travel tip: Be sure to memorize the name of your riverboat. You will never be able to pick it out from the lineup otherwise.]

My camera went missing somewhere between the boat dock and cast off. I don't like to think a fellow traveler snatched it, particularly because we were so intimately spaced on the sleeping deck. Depending on how many passengers are aboard, you will have between two feet and two inches of space between yourself and the perfect stranger next door. Just hope the stranger is indeed perfect.

It helps, too, if he or she does not snore. I do, obnoxiously, according to my doctor. I can be reasonably assured that, if the stranger next door stole my camera, I exacted sweet revenge every night.

Apart from close quarters, these are the memories that stick in our minds about sailing on the Amazon.

Engine trouble. This delayed our departure from Manaus for several hours and required three marine mechanics to sort out the problem. I confess that this created anxiety, as I imagined getting stranded for days out on the immense waterway. Thankfully it didn't happen.

Food. The ship's galley served three hot meals a day for $2 to $5 dollars a plate. Lunch and supper featured rice, beans, a bit of salad and fresh fish from the river. Breakfast plates were identical, except no fish. We washed down the food with assorted tropical fruit juices that I had never before tasted and whose names I can't remember. However, Ben can tell you. He was following a vegan diet at the time and knows all their names, origins and nutritional value.

Cargo. Every so often, we stopped at riverside towns to offload cargo and exchange passengers. These towns depend on riverboats to supply them with life's necessities. Our boat trafficked in toilet paper, soda pop, onions, rice, bottled water and the most tantalizing watermelons you will ever see.

Mosquitoes. A striking recollection about these pests was their absence. Of course, when the boat docked at riverside towns the little critters attacked immediately. But cruising down the middle of the wide river, we neither saw, heard nor felt mosquitoes. They simply couldn't keep up. We slept soundly at night without applying smelly bug spray. Soundly, that is, if the stranger next door did not snore obnoxiously.

Sunsets. The most indelible memory of all was sunset every evening. Neither I nor Barbara nor the kids can recall much of what we did during the daytime. We must have read books, played cards and talked with fellow passengers. I think I did some pushups on the sun deck, but couldn't swear to it.

Ah, but every afternoon when that blazing red ball sank toward the horizon, surrounding itself with every hue of pink, purple and orange, we would stare in hushed amazement. It seemed the entire boat fell silent, except for the purr of the diesel engine. The last bit of the shiny red disc would disappear in a wink and leave us in the brief, equatorial dusk to contemplate for one last moment the immense surroundings of water, sky and tree line. Then night fell suddenly, thick and black, like a heavy blanket spread over the world.

While we're on the subject of the world, let's take a size quiz. (Answers supplied.)

Amazonia

What country of the world has the largest population of Hindus? India.

What country has the largest population of Muslims? Indonesia.

What country has the largest population of Protestant Christians? United States. [Fun fact: Communist China is predicted to soon overtake the U.S.A. in that category. No joke.]

What country has the largest population of Roman Catholics? Brazil.

What country has the largest population of Pentecostals? Brazil.

No joke. If you know anything about the difference between these two branches of Christianity, you understand how remarkable it is that huge populations of these particular faith communities coexist in a single country, even a country as big as Brazil.

Roman Catholicism arrived first, transplanted from Portugal by European conquistadores in 1500. Pentecostalism would come four centuries later, brought by European immigrants to the U.S.A.

Their story is recounted in the intriguing book *The Century of the Holy Spirit* by Vinson Synan. In the first decade of the 20th century, as the Pentecostal movement was being birthed in the U.S., two young Swedes newly arrived from the old country experienced Spirit baptism. Later, Daniel Berg and Gunnar Vingren met at a Pentecostal conference in Chicago and became friends.

Vingren was saving money to enroll in divinity school at the University of Chicago. He later accepted a call to pastor a Swedish Baptist church in South Bend, Indiana. It was there at a Saturday evening service that one of his parishioners prophesied that God was calling Vingren to preach the Good News in "Para." Sometime later Berg visited South Bend and the same parishioner pronounced over him the same prophesy about "Para."

It was clear to Berg and Vingren that they must go to Para, but they had never heard of the place. So, they went to the Chicago Public Library, consulted the World Atlas and discovered that Para was the name of a state in Northeast Brazil. They lost no time securing passage on a ship bound for Belem, the port city at the mouth of the Amazon River.

Berg got a full-time job in a steel mill. The two men lived off his wages so that Vingren could concentrate on planting a church. Their congregation began with 18 members and grew quickly. Berg and Vingren learned that another of their Pentecostal friends from Chicago, Italian immigrant Luigi Franceson, had planted a church in Sao Paulo. They registered the new congregations with the government under the name "Assemblies of God."

A century later, *Assembleia de Deus no Brasil* has grown to 100 thousand congregations with 22.5 million members. Nearly half of all Brazil's evangelical Christians are members of an Assembly of God congregation, making it the largest non-Roman Catholic church in Brazil and the largest Pentecostal denomination in the world. It is seven times larger than the Assemblies of God in the U.S., which is one of the 10 largest Christian denominations in North America.

Modest beginnings, exceptional impact. Who could have imagined what was about to happen on that day when Berg and Vingren visited the Chicago Public Library? Nor would anyone have foreseen that, in addition to its many sizeable attributes, the Amazon would add this one: Birthplace of a massive Jesus Movement.

The only thing those two young Swedes did was to obey the voice of God. No plan, no budget, no outstanding qualifications. Just simple, radical obedience.

God did the rest.

After all, if He can turn a trickling stream in the Andes into the mighty Amazon, imagine what He can do with a few people who are willing to obey the move of his Spirit.

Endless in Brazil

If you plan to travel the length of Brazil as we did on the Epic, you need to know that it is the longest country in the world from north to south, equivalent to the distance from Alaska to Hawaii. And at its widest east-west point, Brazil is a bit broader than the continental U.S. Traveling overland can seem endless.

Here's the good news. Brazil is the only country in the world that has both the Equator and the Tropic of Capricorn running through it, which means you can go almost anywhere in the country at any time of year in shorts and flip flops.

Shorts and flip flops appear to be the national costume. Perhaps it is because of the perennial warm weather, perhaps because of Brazilians' laid-back approach to life or perhaps because 70 percent of the population lives near the coast and must constantly be prepared for a day at the beach. The phenomenon certainly warrants careful research.

Other aspects of Brazilian life deserve examination, as well. For instance, why has it outperformed every other nation on earth by winning five World Cups in *futebol* (the sport known as soccer in the U.S.)? Is it because Brazil's professional players only have one name, like Pelé, Ronaldinho or Neymar? Or do Brazil's players use only one name because they have won five World Cups?

Perhaps their prowess is due to their penchant for foot volley (*futevolei* in Portuguese), a sport invented on the beaches of Rio de Janeiro. As the name implies, futevolei players use only their feet to get the ball over the net and back. This fascinating technique allows them to play two of their favorite games at once: volleyball, which some consider the National Sport, and futebol, which many consider the National Religion.

These are but a few of many fascinating issues to explore. Brazil could absorb several lifetimes of observation and still keep its secrets. The most biodiverse country on the planet, it holds world records for the most species of plants, freshwater fish and mammals. Heretofore unknown species of birds, bugs and reptiles are regularly being discovered in its vast jungles.

The Epic provided us time and access to experience many unique things about Brazil, but even then, we barely scratched the surface.

The riverboat dropped us at Itaituba, a city on the banks of the Tapajos 150 miles from where this enormous river meets the Amazon. (If you are confused here, please see the previous chapter.) Barbara and I had been asked to teach intensive classes in Counseling and Church History to Bible institute students there. Meanwhile, Ben, Molly and Lindsey, lucky ducks, spent the week helping with the mango harvest at the *Hacienda Maloquinha*.

Maloquinha is a special place. One thousand acres of cattle ranch/retreat center/riverside resort, it sits 11 miles out of town on a rutted dirt road. On weekends Maloquinha opens to the public and hundreds of city dwellers make the bone-jarring, half hour commute to bathe in the warm Tapajos, dine on fresh fare in the farm's restaurant and play futebol and volei amidst Maloquinha's huge mango trees.

It was November, when the trees are in full production and drop mangoes by the hundreds every day. The first item on the agenda each morning at Maloquinha was to don hard hats (to deflect falling mangoes) and collect the fruit in big canvas bags.

Ben, Molly and Lindsey collected mangoes and helped with farm chores, laundry and housekeeping. Ben fed the *tambaqui* in Maloquinha's fish ponds, which also held two or three large *piraracú*, the most feared fish in the Amazon. One weekend when Barbara and I visited the farm, Ben showed us why.

A six-foot long, 200-pound piraracú had settled lazily below the pond's feeding pier. The big fellow looked the very image of a docile gentle giant. Then Ben dropped a piece of fresh meat in the direction of its nose and *Wham*!

We didn't actually see what happened. The gigantic fish attacked too fast for the naked eye to follow and sucked in the prey with a blast like a shotgun. Within half a second, the fresh meat and the huge piraracú had disappeared beneath gentle ripples on the surface, leaving this pale-faced, drop-jawed visitor staring down in disbelief from the feeding pier.

This was but one experience that made our stay in Itaituba memorable. Another was reconnecting with Oreste and Marlene Greiner, a couple that I had met in Curitiba on my first visit to Brazil in 1974. All three of us were college students at that time. A year later, Oreste and Marlene graduated and moved to the Amazon to plant churches, an enterprise they still pursue at this writing.

When it was time for us to leave, the Greiners shared our itinerary with friends and colleagues who lived along our route. For a week, we traveled south on a line roughly parallel to Brazil's western border, through Novo Progreso, Sinop, Cuiaba and Campo Grande, ending up in Marechal Rondón. We covered most of the 1,700 miles in bus seats. The long days and longer nights left us groggy and craving showers, a hot meal and somewhere to stretch our cramped legs.

Invariably, we found a family awaiting us at the bus station. Mind you, these folks worked full-time jobs while planting churches, yet they still found time to take foreigners into their homes. They gave us beds, cooked for us and even did laundry. "Hospitality" took on a new meaning.

"Geography" took on a new meaning, as well. Midway through this southward trek we reached Cuiaba, Brazil's hottest city. West of it lies the Pantanal, the world's largest system of wetlands. Researchers have discovered more plant and animal species here than in the Amazon jungle itself, ranking the Pantanal as the world's most biodiverse ecosystem.

To the east of Cuiaba lies the *Chapada dos Guimarães*. A high tableland rising abruptly out of the savannah, the Chapada inspires awe at first sight. It also inspired the movie "The Lost World," a science fiction adventure featuring dinosaurs and other dangerous leviathans that explorers encounter atop the uncharted plateau.

To date, no dinosaurs have been found on the Chapada. However, the plateau is high enough to block prevailing winds from reaching Cuiaba. Denied the cooling breezes, the city registers temperatures above 100 degrees Fahrenheit for much of the year, earning Cuiaba its unenviable reputation as the hottest city in the hottest country in the Americas.

The Chapada is noteworthy for yet another phenomenon. It sits on the exact geographical center of South America. When we discovered that we had reached this milestone, we asked Lindsey to snap a photo of us celebrating the achievement, in midair.

We were able to do all this courtesy of Fabio and Marli Cristiani, church planters in Cuiaba who housed us, fed us and even loaned us their car to explore the Chapada. As I said, hospitality took on a new meaning, and church planters are among the most hospitable folks you will ever meet.

Perhaps that is because church planting is best done as a team. For example, the Cristianis had moved to Cuiaba a few years prior to team up with Ivan and Normandi Mouro to plant a church in the city. The Mouros had moved to Cuiaba from Itaituba, where they had been part of a church planted by our friends, Oreste and Marlene.

That church grew large from humble beginnings. Itaituba consisted of only four city blocks in 1975, the year the Greiners moved from Curitiba to Amazonia. The church began holding meetings at the busiest place in town: the wharf where riverboats arrive from cities downriver to unload passengers and freight.

Four years later, Edgar and Cilli Henke arrived in Itaituba. They only planned to stay a year in order to give the Greiners a breather, but the pressing needs of the frontier town and the opportunity to sow the gospel in virgin soil changed their minds. They decided to stay for life. The decision surprised no one who knew the Henkes and their passion for serving Jesus.

I had the privilege of meeting Edgar and Cilli in Curitiba, in 1974. They were directing the Bible training institute where Oreste and Marlene were studying. I was part of a team of American students that came to help build classrooms at the school. Edgar Henke, himself a builder by trade, supervised our work between his administrative duties as director of the institute.

Mr. Henke came from a family of German immigrants who raised him to value hard work. Solidly built with coal black hair and a thick, matching mustache, he exuded the sort of demeanor that causes people to hush when he enters the room.

One day I was laying brick for a classroom wall. My buddy Will was working nearby. We were horsing around as college guys sometimes do when, without warning, Will grabbed me from behind and pinned my arms to my sides. He was a linebacker on the college football team so maybe his tackling instinct kicked in. Anyway, we struggled, I tripped on some brick trash and we both collapsed in a heap, taking down the newly laid brick wall with us.

We sat up in the swirling dust and stared at each other. We were toast. A careless act like this, committed on foreign soil, was certainly a deportable offense. But the only thing for it was to go to the Director, own up to our stupidity and take the medicine.

Edgar Henke was sitting behind his desk when we walked in and, through an interpreter, described the incident. He listened quietly, expressionless except for a raised eyebrow here and a fleeting smile there. We apologized profusely, pledged to cover all damages and swore to behave ourselves if he would just give us another chance and not kick us out of Brazil.

Mr. Henke sat thinking it over for a moment, a very long moment, it seemed to me.

"Thank you, boys, for coming in and telling me this," came his reply through the interpreter. "I accept your apology. And don't worry, you need not pay anything."

Then he looked straight at us and added, "Remember, these things happen even in the best of families."

The knot in my stomach loosened. I managed a weak smile and a mumbled "thank you, Sir," and we left the office. I was so relieved that I hardly realized what had just happened.

What happened was this: Edgar Henke, being the wise and dignified man that he was, chastised us appropriately without destroying our dignity. Talk about class. That proved to be the only conversation I ever had with the man, but I never forgot it. That's what happens, you know, when you have a close encounter with a great leader.

Edgar Henke's career in Itaituba demonstrated the truly great leader he was. With Cilli at his side and the Greiners as coworkers, it did not take long for extraordinary things to happen.

To begin with, the team figured out that the property at the wharf was better suited for doing business than planting a church, so they leased it to shopkeepers and used the proceeds to move to one of the new neighborhoods springing up on the edge of town.

The place was thick with children, some of them from dysfunctional families, others with no family at all. So instead of a chapel, Henke designed and built the first Community Integrated Center for Minors, a safe place where kids could play, have a nutritious meal and get help with school work. The Center concept became the prototype for planting churches in Itaituba.

Henke encountered idle teenagers with no job skills, so he opened an industrial shop to teach them furniture making and construction trades. When circumstances came together to acquire the Hacienda Maloquinha, Edgar set about teaching them agricultural and hospitality skills at the ranch.

In 1996, doctors installed a pacemaker in Edgar Henke and told him he should take it easy from now on and rest. His answer: "I will rest once I get to Heaven." He continued to help plant churches and build schools. In 2001, Henke oversaw construction of Bethel Clinic, a facility that provides medical services to low-income families.

When Edgar Henke died 26 years after arriving in Itaituba, the city had grown to 100,000 residents. Fellow citizens paid their respects with one of the largest funeral processions in Itaituba's history. Police officers and firemen marched in dress uniform and the mayor presented Cilli Henke with an award honoring her husband's service to the community.

Of course, that is not the end of the story. A life well-lived serving Jesus has impact long after the servant's departure. Oreste and Marlene and their colleagues are still busy planting churches, now primarily along the Trans-Amazon Highway and in distant cities like Cuiaba. These congregations have collectively baptized several thousand new believers. Their numbers continue to grow.

I suspect that what started at the wharf in Itaituba in the 1970s is likely to keep changing lives and transforming communities in Brazil for years to come. As history shows, genuine Jesus movements can indeed be endless.

Endless in Brazil

Big water

We ended our long trek through Brazil at one of the Seven Wonders of the Natural World. The Cataracts of Iguazu straddle Brazil's southern border with Argentina. Of all the borders in South America, this one is undoubtedly the most breathtaking.

Anybody who gets within a thousand miles of them should take time to experience Iguazu Falls.

Wider than Africa's famed Victoria Falls and nearly twice the height of Niagara, Iguazu is actually composed of many individual cataracts--275 to be exact--that plunge over sheer cliffs into a narrow canyon 260 feet below.

When you go, be sure to wear your swim suit because when you approach the thundering water you get drenched with perpetual mist, and love it.

Travelers carry on a perpetual debate about which side of the falls offers the best visitor experience. If you choose the vantage point in Brazil, you get unhindered panoramas of the cataracts from the cliffside causeway that runs the length of the canyon. The trek ends at the bottom of the massive Devil's Throat cataract. Only half the water of the Iguazu River plunges over the Devil's Throat, yet it is enough to fill two Olympic-size swimming pools every second.

Visitors to Argentina's Iguazu National Park must walk a country mile from the park entrance to their first glimpse of the falls, but the hike through lush tropical forest is well worth it. Along the way you might see toucans, parrots and others of the 400 bird species that live here. You might also come across iguanas, monkeys or, very occasionally, a giant anteater.

A park animal you will most certainly encounter is the coati, South America's version of the raccoon. Once scarce and shy, they now roam the trails in menacing herds. Do not feed them, park rangers tell you. Actually, you won't need to, the coatis feed themselves. They have learned how to poke their pointy noses into bags and backpacks to snatch snacks, and they can pounce on unsuspecting picnickers and gobble up lunch in seconds.

But even these rascals can't spoil the pleasure of roaming Iguazu's water wonderland. I have been to the falls probably seven or eight times over the years,

Big water

and every visit is as delightful as the first one. For me, one of most unforgettable experiences at Iguazu is to stand on Argentina's causeway atop the Devil's Throat, drenched in milky mist thrown up from the falls. The thunderous roar makes conversation impossible and you try not to think about what would happen if you fell into the terrifying torrent. But the tension fades as you notice hundreds of butterflies fluttering around the heads of the spectators and landing on their shoulders.

When you visit Iguazu, plan to spend several days enjoying Argentina's fascinating province of Misiones. The inhabitants are called "*misioneros*" ("missionaries" in English), which is one reason we feel so much at home here. Why would we not, when mingling with 1.3 million fellow missionaries, the highest concentration of us in the world?

We feel at home in Misiones for other reasons, the most important being the many friends who house and feed us when we visit. Our hosts pamper us with daily barbecues featuring Argentina's famous beef. They have also taught us to savor Argentina's national pastime:

friendly conversation carried on while sipping *yerba mate*.

If you have never experienced yerba mate, I will try, and likely fail, to describe this unique beverage. No, that's not right; yerba mate is more than a beverage. It's an institution.

The recipe is simple enough. You start with a small gourd or wooden cup, the *mate* [MAH-tay], and fill it two-thirds full with *yerba* [YAIR-bah], crushed kiln-dried leaves from a small tree that grows in the red soil of the Southern Cone and, I'm told, nowhere else in the world. Then you insert a strainer-tipped metal straw into the mate and pour hot water over the yerba. Let it soak for a moment, then take a pull.

It's best not to sip alone. This stuff is made to share. Couples, entire families and groups of friends will usually share the mate, recharging it with hot water after each sip and passing it around the circle several times. According to protocol, you are not to say "gracias" (thank you) until you are finished sipping. In yerba mate culture, this is the polite way to signal to your host that you want no more.

Watching a person take their first sip of yerba mate always reveals the range of human responses to new and unusual flavors. For example, if the sip elicits startled surprise followed by something like, "Wow! That's potent stuff!", then this person will probably try the beverage again, and again, until he or she develops a taste for it. Other first-time sippers just stare ahead, deadpan, then wordlessly withdraw the metal straw. This is the noncommittal, let-me think-this-over response. Watch this person closely to see whether he or she takes a second sip or firmly says "gracias" when it is offered.

Finally, there is the "Oh my gosh! What just hit my mouth?" reaction, typically accompanied by eyes tight shut and an explosive ejection of the metal straw. This person will under no circumstances accept a second sip. Protocol dictates that he or she should say a polite "gracias" to the host, but invariably it comes out "YUCK!"

To appreciate the vital importance of mate culture, I suggest you take a tour of a yerba processing plant. One of our favorites is a mom-and-pop operation that follows the age-old technique of drying the leaves in a wood-fired kiln and aging them in burlap. This is the process invented by the Guarani, the first inhabitants of the Southern Cone. They shared their secret with the first Europeans to arrive in their part of the world and yerba was on its way to becoming the valuable commodity that it is today.

Those first Europeans were members of the Society of Jesus, popularly known as Jesuits. The Society established the mission of

Big water

San Ignacio Guazú in present-day Paraguay a full decade before the Mayflower arrived on the coast of Massachusetts. From that base, the Jesuits expanded missionary outreach to territories in Brazil, Argentina and Bolivia. Their considerable influence on Argentina is what inspired the name of the province of Misiones.

By 1750, nearly 200 thousand native Americans were living in Jesuit mission centers spread across the Southern Cone. Called "reductions", the missions gathered Guarani families into communal settlements to teach them agriculture, literacy, cloth making, carpentry, arts, music and Catholicism. In many of the reductions Jesuit fathers built grand chapels and cathedrals, architectural wonders that still survive and never fail to impress.

Sadly, the missions themselves failed to survive. When European colonists began to populate the region, opposition to the Jesuit missions mounted. Plantation owners coveted the choice land cultivated by Guarani communities. Slave traders resented the Jesuits because they protected the natives from being trafficked.

Influential Spanish and Portuguese colonists lobbied their respective governments to rein in the Jesuits. They falsely claimed that the fathers forced the Guarani into slavery and were amassing huge fortunes from their labor. They said the missionaries employed threats and physical abuse to confine the Guarani to their reductions.

None of these charges were true, but in the end, it made no difference. European economics and politics, aided by Vatican jealousy of the Jesuit order, produced the intended effect. Portugal expelled the Jesuits from Brazil in 1759. Eight years later, Spain ordered their expulsion from the rest of the Americas.

If this story sounds vaguely familiar, it could be because you have seen the movie "The Mission." In the film, Jeremy Irons portrays a pioneering Jesuit missionary and Robert De Niro a repentant slave trader. The two join forces to defend the Guarani from rapacious European colonists. Their effort is doomed to failure, of course.

The plot of The Mission is tragic, but the scenery is stunning. I should mention that the movie won an Oscar for best cinematography. It was filmed at Iguazu so you could say that, along with the other accolades, the Falls are now an Oscar-winning Wonder of the Natural World.

In the mid-twentieth century, history repeated itself when a new wave of missionary outreach spread through indigenous communities in South America. Working through organizations such as Wycliffe Bible Translators, New Tribes Mission, the Swiss Indian Mission and YWAM, evangelical missionaries began to engage aboriginal tribes, many of whom had little or no contact with the outside world.

In contrast to their counterparts in the era of European colonialism, the new missionaries had not come to "civilize" native Americans or to introduce them to "modern ways" developed in Western cultures. Their purpose was simply to offer them the gospel of Jesus in understandable language in hopes they might want to become his followers.

Sadly, the new missionaries encountered far fewer native Americans than did their colonial counterparts. Since the arrival of Europeans, the indigenous population has suffered huge losses. Researchers estimate that 90 percent of the original Americans, 55 million persons, died of smallpox, measles or influenza after 1492. The inhabitants of Amazon numbered five million then; they are less than 200,000 today. In this century alone, 100 entire tribes have ceased to exist.

The technical term for this is "ethnocide," the death of a culture, and it is catastrophic. As happens when a species becomes extinct, the world loses a part of itself. An irreplaceable language disappears. A unique way of life dies.

Like the Jesuits, today's missionaries to native Americans face determined opposition to their work. Anthropologists, human rights activists and businessmen are among those lobbying for their expulsion.

According to their detractors, these missionaries are committing ethnocide in their endeavor to Christianize tribal peoples.

These allegations sound eerily similar to those leveled against the Jesuits 300 years ago. Modern missionaries continue to face charges of enriching themselves through exploitation of slave labor. Some have even been accused of illegally mining gold on isolated tribal lands. Impartial investigations have yet to uncover a shred of evidence to support these claims, nevertheless the popular perception persists that missionaries are bad news for native Americans.

An impartial look at the facts suggests just the opposite. Tribes that are involved with Christian missionaries are making remarkable comebacks.

For example, the Arabela tribe of Peru numbered only 50

individuals in 1954 and lived in virtual slavery to rubber traders. That year, missionaries arrived and commenced translating the Bible into the Arabela language. The tribe has since rebounded to more than 300 persons.

Wycliffe Bible Translators first contacted Bolivia's 100 surviving Chacobos in the 1960s. The tribe has since tripled in size. Observers attribute this to the Chacobos' conscious affirmation of their language and culture, a result that typically arises from the process of Bible translation.

The Paumari of Brazil have also staged a comeback. Numbering 150 tribal members in 1964, the Paumari are more than 600 today, mainly because their acceptance of Christianity countered the menace of alcoholism, a social ailment that speeds cultural disintegration. Later on, their newfound faith prompted them to reject an even deadlier Western vice: cocaine trafficking.

These are but a few of scores of case studies that indicate the positive effect of Christian missions on aboriginal peoples. Contrary to popular perception, missionary engagement effectively breaks the cycle of ethnocide. The indigenous person's beliefs about God and the spiritual world change, but for the most part this does not alter their lifestyle. These groups still dress in the same fashion, hunt and fish according to custom, and live in traditional dwellings. Often their cultural self-image is strengthened when they understand that a loving Creator made them uniquely as they are and commissioned them to act as stewards over their ancestral homeland.

With all due respect to the critics, this trend sounds like good news to me. You might even say it ranks as a Wonder of the Natural World.

Hunting ground

If you have followed our Epic ramblings this far, then you know we made a lot of memories. One that stands out to me for sheer terror was a brutal assault we suffered in the Argentine Chaco.

We were attacked by monster mosquitoes.

You will be able to relate to this if you have tramped through southern swamplands, desperately swatting the little devils in order to stay alive. Or, if you have gone fishing in the Canadian north woods in summer, when clouds of ravenous no-see-ums chew on every inch of exposed flesh. Only if you've suffered like this do you truly know about life-threatening insects.

But take my word for it, Chaco mosquitoes are world champs, no kidding.

We narrowly escaped death-by-suction one day when we drove 20 miles into the bush to photograph a historic and now abandoned chapel. We had no sooner stepped out of our minivan when squadrons of thirsty mozzies zeroed in at Mach One. Black and beefy with bodies shaped like buffalo, these creatures did not hum, they screamed like fighter jets.

We beat a hasty retreat to the minivan, diving inside just in time to escape serious bloodshed. As we took photos of the sacred building through the windshield, hundreds of the crazed kamikazes slammed against the glass, trying to get at us. It was pure Alfred Hitchcock horror.

I am fully aware that you will consider all this farfetched exaggeration, unless you have visited the Chaco and personally confronted its malicious insect population. For example, the Juanita beetle secretes a poison on your skin that blisters into a moldy infection. Biting gnats, indifferent to repellent and small enough to penetrate window screens, leave red wounds that itch for days. Another bug resembling rye seed swarms around light bulbs to drop dead *en masse* onto the dining room table, or between the keys of your computer or, most annoying of all, down your shirt.

I'm convinced the bugs are partly responsible for giving the Chaco its name. "Chaco" comes from a Quechua word that means "a place to hunt." Anthropologists think Native Americans named it for the rich variety of game present in the region. Personally, I believe that the earliest humans went to the Chaco *only* to hunt, but had better sense than to make their homes there.

Three countries, Bolivia, Paraguay and Argentina share the Gran Chaco, an area equal in size to South Dakota, Nebraska and Kansas put together. These are three of the flattest states in the U.S.A. and that is exactly what the Chaco is. Except that the Chaco is flatter, so flat that no rivers flow through vast stretches of its plains. Rain stays put at the very spot it falls from the sky, pooling ankle- or knee-deep for days. Farm families must endure flooded gardens, outhouses and living rooms until the hard clay soil allows the water to slowly seep underground.

Granted, rain is only an occasional occurrence. If it rains, farmers can produce cotton, soybeans, sunflowers and melons in the Chaco. However, drought is the norm. Some last as long as six months, others as long as three years. Summer temperatures can reach 120°F for days on end. Farming the Chaco, you can imagine, is not for the meek.

Nobody even tried farming here until about a hundred years ago. *Chaqueños*, as inhabitants are known, have faced up to their severe environment with severe realism. Hardy pioneers gave names to their towns like Rio Muerto (Dead River), Monte Quemado (Burnt Brush) and Pampa del Infierno (Plain of Hell).

Hunting ground

By the way, there's a great little diner called The Two Brothers where you can stop for lunch in the Plain of Hell. But you may not want to stay for supper.

As you can guess, Chaqueños are some of the toughest people on the planet. They are also among the most hospitable. We found this out while spending a week with the Borke family who were pastors of a church in Coronel du Graty. Actually, just Barbara, Ben and I spent the week there. Molly and Lindsey decided to forego the whole Chaco experience and took off instead for Buenos Aires.

The congregation in Coronel du Graty was composed chiefly of descendants of farmers who immigrated here from Central and Eastern Europe in the early 1900s. German speakers in the main, they considered the Chaco something of a promised land compared to the countries plagued by war, poverty and political turmoil that they left behind.

Hard-working and thrifty, Chaqueños are also generous. When they heard the pastor was hosting guests from out of town, homemade pickles, potato salad, cakes, cookies, and sides of pork and goat appeared for the table. We passed a remarkably pleasant week, sheltering from the heat and bugs in the Borke's comfortable home and enjoying frequent barbecues in their shady backyard.

When it came time to leave, Molly and Lindsey rendezvoused with us at the bus station in Saenz Peña for the overnight trip to the Bolivian border. Though less than 24 hours in duration, their Chaco experience lived up to expectations, as this entry from Molly's journal attests.

"We left Monday afternoon to embark on a very looong journey. Around 2:00 a.m., we arrived in a small town and were informed that we had just missed our connecting bus. The next one did not arrive until 7:30 am. In any other town, this news would not have been so bad, but we had just arrived in the creepiest (literally) bus station we had seen yet.

"Large beetles covered the parking lot in a carpet of black, squirming bugs that crunched under our feet. You literally had to dance to keep from having one climb up your leg. As we looked on in dismay, a stray dog lapped up a few of them in an attempt at a nutritious dinner.

"Fortunately, we still had two hammocks with us. Dad and Lindsey found a place to hang them. Mom and I lay down on a sheet on the concrete platform far from the beetles, hoping to catch a bit of shut eye. Ben stayed awake most of the time, diligently keeping watch over our bags and logging our adventure in his journal. I awoke to a swarm of white gnats and many curious eyes watching me from across the street."

Lest we leave the impression that the Chaco produces only insects, you should know that it contains nearly 3,500 varieties of plants, 99.9 percent of which have thorns. The legendary quebracho tree yields hardwood so tough that, like diamonds, it shatters to pieces if not cut correctly.

Animals common in other parts of South America prowl the forests, including the jaguar, peccary, deer, tapir and howler monkey. Bird watchers come from around the world in hopes of spotting some of the 500 species of birds that nest here. The renowned British theologian John Stott eagerly accepted invitations to lead Bible conferences in Paraguay, I am told, so that he could afterward spend a few days in the Chaco indulging his passion for birdwatching.

Granted, theologians are scarce in the Chaco. So are the Pentecostal megachurches so common these days in Latin America's big cities. That is probably because there are no big cities in the Chaco.

Nevertheless, there does exist here a unique expression of

Hunting ground

Christianity that attracts interest from around the world. I am talking about the Mennonite colonies.

First, some context. About a hundred years ago, Bolivia and Paraguay fought a war in the Chaco. It seems inconceivable that nations would sacrifice their best and brightest for this desolate terrain, but that is exactly what happened. The Gran Chaco War claimed 100,000 lives, making it the costliest combat fought on South American soil in the 20th century.

Like most wars, the reasons why it happened are fuzzy. Borders between Paraguay and Bolivia were themselves fuzzy, having been demarcated by Spanish law during colonial times. Just which parts of the Chaco belonged to which country was constantly in dispute, provoking perpetual skirmishes between forward military posts. The conflict exploded into all-out war in 1932 with the Battle of Boquerón.

Like a lot of wars, outsiders meddled in the conflict. Bolivia's commander in chief, General Hans Kundt, was a German veteran of WW1. His tactics caused unnecessarily high casualties and he was soon replaced. But European involvement continued. Arms dealers from Czechoslovakia, England, Germany, France and Italy supplied guns to both armies. The Chaco became a sort of firing range for field testing weapons later used in WW2.

Like many wars, its outcome was inconclusive and disappointing. In 1935, Argentina mediated a ceasefire and then brokered the 1938 permanent peace treaty. That agreement granted Paraguay three-quarters of the northern Chaco, nearly doubling the size of the country. Bolivia's war prize was a land corridor to the Paraguay River and the right to construct a port for ocean-going ships, a dream that has yet to be realized.

Like all wars, this one led to tragic loss of life and great economic hardship that could in no way justify a rationale for fighting it. Paraguay fought to acquire vast oil reserves believed to lie beneath the Chaco. But none were discovered when the war ended. For Bolivia, the Chaco War set in motion a decades-long cycle of political instability that hindered the country's economic development and social progress. The disaster led Eusebio Ayala to lament, "It is unfortunate that two poor nations would use their limited resources to destroy each other."

It was in this period of war that Mennonites planted their colonies in Paraguay. Mennonites are known mainly for their plain ways, plain clothes and fabulous home cooking. Yet they, too, are acquainted with conflict and loss. For centuries they suffered unrelenting religious persecution in Europe.

Their troubles go all the way back to the Protestant Reformation. The most radical of the reformers, they adamantly objected to the custom of infant baptism. This earned them the derogatory nickname "Anabaptists." Their insistence that the church be separate from the state invited the wrath of princes and priests alike. Their radical stance on theological and social issues of the day led to thousands dying as martyrs.

But it was their commitment to pacifism that caused Mennonites the greatest grief. Church leaders negotiated agreements with one European ruler after another to exempt their men from going to war, only to see subsequent governments nullify the pacts. When that happened, Mennonite pacifists faced the options of bearing arms, serving jail time or worse. So, they uprooted their families and moved on.

Eventually Mennonites cast their eye on the New World and its infant democracies. By and large, they found these countries refreshingly tolerant of their ideals. Paraguay accepted the first group of 1,740 Mennonite colonists in 1927 and

Hunting ground

settled them in the deep Chaco. They were the first persons of European descent ever to live there and attempt to farm the land. Initial hardships claimed more than 120 lives; 60 families gave up and moved to Canada. Yet the colony survived and eventually thrived. Known today as Filadelfia, it is the largest and wealthiest population center in the deep Chaco.

More Mennonite colonies took root in the 1930s and 40s, as word got around about the cheap land and tolerant public officials. Paraguay allowed the colonies to establish their own schools and teach classes in German, a hallmark of the Mennonite community. The colonies multiplied and flourished.

Economists affirm that Mennonites in Paraguay today enjoy a quality of life on par with Spaniards. Their achievements have benefited the entire economy of Paraguay, propelling the small country into sixth place among the world's beef exporters. The 40 thousand Mennonite colonists make up less than one percent of the population, yet account for seven percent of the country's GDP.

What is their secret? "Without faith in God and Jesus Christ, this would not have been possible," Patrick Friesen, leader of the agricultural cooperative in Filadelfia, told a visiting journalist in 2012.

There is yet another secret to their story. Paraguayan officials initially encouraged Mennonites to colonize the Chaco in order to counter Bolivian incursions into the region. They calculated that they could legitimately claim ownership of the Gran Chaco only if they settled it with their own citizens. The fact that the chosen settlers were pacifists was not lost on Paraguayan officials. That made them an ideal buffer between opposing armies, a sort of non-violent, peace-keeper force.

It must have worked, because Bolivia and Paraguay have been at peace now for nearly a hundred years. Perhaps that is also due to the fact that Mennonites have built colonies in Bolivia on the northern edge of the Chaco, in effect creating a double buffer of peace keepers.

It occurs to me that this expression of Christianity is just what the Chaco needed. Taking into account what Jesus said in the Beatitudes about peacemakers, that "they shall be call the children of God," I reckon the Mennonites have been a real blessing to the Chaco.

And if any place on earth could use a blessing, this hot, harsh, dry hunting ground is certainly one.

Home in the Llajta

A plaque on our wall says, "Home is where you hang your heart." In four decades of marriage, Barbara and I have made our home in Kentucky, Costa Rica, Bolivia, Florida, and Indiana. But the place where we have hung our hearts the longest is Cochabamba.

The Epic Journey ended in Cochabamba 89 days, 12,634 miles and 12 border crossings after we departed Indianapolis. Our bus ride through the Argentine Chaco brought us to the banks of the Pilcomayo River. We crossed in a motorboat to Bermejo, Bolivia, and presented our papers at the immigration office. Ben confessed that he was feeling a bit nervous, unsure of how it would go for him and Molly because they were Bolivian citizens traveling on U.S. passports. He also fretted that the authorities might hassle him over his draft status, since he had not served the mandatory year in the army required of all Bolivian young men.

"However, the most honest and efficient border official I´ve ever met stamped us in, no worries, and welcomed us home," Ben wrote in his journal. "I can't lie, it was an emotional moment."

From Bermejo we traveled in a shuttle van to the city of Tarija. We swerved and skidded on the winding highway for the entire four hours in order to dodge mounted cowboys and the cattle herds they were driving to summer pasture. By then, I confess that *I* was a bit nervous. First thing next morning, we splurged on airline tickets to Cochabamba. I decided that a one-hour flight in lieu of another 20-hour bus ride was just the way to celebrate the last leg of the Epic and, I can't lie, make it home in one piece.

"Cochabamba" [Koh-cha-BAHM-ba] is a compound Quechua name meaning "the flat place with water." Its 16th century founders located the city inside a gentle bend of the River Rocha near a marshy lake, thus ensuring a constant water supply. Cochabamba natives fondly use another Quechua word for the city which you won't find on maps. "Llajta" [YAHK-tah] loosely translated can mean "town" or "people" or even "my people." To those of us lucky enough to live here, the Llajta is simply "the home town."

The evening our flight landed in the Llajta, the home town soccer team faced off against a menacing rival in a do-or-die playoff match. Ben recorded the events.

"Felix Capriles Stadium was bursting at the seams, everybody cheering for our club, Wilsterman. We rushed to the stadium in time to catch the second half. Games here are dramatic and this one did not fail to impress. Lindsey was crushed under several youths trying to catch a gift ball kicked into the stands. A player from the rival team was knocked to the ground by a bottle thrown from the bleachers. A young man punched the main referee in the face, then managed to wiggle free of riot police and escape into the mass of fans. The local side pulled through with an impressive goal to win and we made a mad dash to the exit before 30,000 celebrating *Cochabambinos* poured out into the streets.

"I'm still in a state of shock, it doesn't quite feel real. Because we have been in transit for the last three months, the idea of permanence seems unnatural. But before getting lost in the excitement, I would like to pen some words of closure to the journey.

"No words could describe the deep GRATITUDE I feel for the places we encountered, and for those who hosted us, interacted with us, and opened up their hearts, homes and refrigerators. They taught many a lesson about hospitality. I'm still humbled by the people who vacated their bedrooms so we could occupy them, covered extra shifts at their workplace to show us around and refused gas money."

For myself, I experienced similar feelings, but expressed them differently. For days, I went around humming the old Simon and Garfunkel tune, "Gee, but it's great to be back home! Home is where I wanna be-ye . . ."

We didn't have an actual home to come home to. Before leaving for the States a year and a half earlier, Barbara and I had moved out of our rented apartment and warehoused all our belongings. No worries, our good friends Paul and Kattia Jones were away on furlough and loaned us their spacious house until we could relocate. We arrived just days before Christmas, so our good friends Graham and Lori Porter graciously hosted us for the holidays, stuffing us with scrumptious food and letting us take long naps on the sofa between meals.

Did I mention that good friends are what make the Llajta, well, the Llajta?

Cochabamba sits in a wide valley 8,500 feet above sea level, which at this latitude gives it a climate much like California's. It supports palm trees and pine trees equally well and has only two annual seasons: wet and dry. Intermittent rains fall between December and May, none falls during the rest of the year. The most constant element of the weather is golden sunshine.

California gets its rain during the winter, but because seasons are reversed, Cochabamba's rain falls in the summer. It's a subtle but important difference that means our weather is neither as cool nor as hot as California's. Daytime temperatures range between the low 70s in winter and the low 80s in summer. Like other cities located in high Andes valleys--Medellin, Cuenca, Cusco, Salta--the climate in the Llajta is described as "Eternal Spring."

It may sound too good to be true, but it is. Sometimes Barbara and I, while strolling through a shady park or sitting on our veranda, will look at one another and say, "You know, on a day like this, why would you ever think of living anywhere else?"

Few tourists come to Bolivia and fewer come to Cochabamba. The Llajta offers no must-see attractions like Lake Titicaca, or Tiawanaku or the Uyuni Salt Flats, sites several hours distant. The shortage of tourists does not bother locals, however, who quip that Cochabamba is a great place to live but you wouldn't want to have to visit here.

Barbara and I were barely beyond our honeymoon when we first arrived in Cochabamba. Our three eldest children, Sarah, Benjamin and Molly were born in San Pedro Clinic when it was little more than a stately house with delivery rooms and a nursery. We raised the kids their first years across the street from Felix Capriles Stadium, which probably infected them with soccer fever. Carmen, our youngest, joined the family when we were furloughing in the U.S. She is the only one of us with blue eyes. This sometimes puzzles Bolivians until we explain, tongue in cheek, that it is because she was born in the middle of a cold Indiana winter.

Lest I create the impression that we settled in Cochabamba because of its ideal climate, stunning natural beauty and engaging lifestyle, I should mention that our missionary agency sent Barbara and I here to replace Dr. Homer and Elvira Firestone, who were about to retire. We were chosen for the assignment, we later learned, largely because we were young and healthy and therefore expected to endure the rigors of the Andes. Right off the bat we learned that whatever our other credentials, we would never be able to fill the Firestones' shoes.

Homer grew up in the Oklahoma Dust Bowl and trained as a Navy pilot in WW2. He earned a Ph.D. in Anthropology and conducted pioneer research on Bolivia's aboriginal languages. Elvira used her B.S. degree in Nursing to deliver babies and treat illnesses for country folk who seldom saw a doctor. When the couple became "tentmakers" [missionaries who support themselves through self-employment], she opened Bolivia's first-ever Chiropractic clinic.

Homer and Elvira had been working in Bolivia nearly 40 years by the time Barbara and I arrived. We had the good fortune to spend our first year with them, soaking up their wisdom. Homer tutored us on his methods for growing successful Jesus movements among Quechua- and Aymara-speaking *campesinos* [Native American peasant farmers]. His simple, three-step strategy produces extraordinary results if correctly applied.

Step One: Show up. "Don't forget," Homer constantly reminded us, "ninety percent of the job is just showing up." Simple as it sounds, showing up to remote villages in the high Andes or dense Amazon jungle presents some challenges. Travel often meant hours of bouncing over precarious mountain roads, then more hours hiking over rugged trails. The risk of coming down with *sorojchi* [altitude sickness] or ingesting parasites was constant. But an opportunity to present the gospel to campesinos hungry to know God always made showing up worthwhile.

Step two: Don't plan. "Plans always change, so why make them in the first place?" Homer pointed out. "Besides, God already has a plan and it's far better than anything we could come up with. Best look for God's plan and follow it." The usefulness of this advice when operating in a foreign culture should be obvious, especially to those of us who live by faith and not by sight. But not so. I once gave a four-hour lecture on Homer's strategy to a university Missions class. When I finished, the professor pointedly reminded the students that their term project entitled "My Five-year Plan" would be due the following week. Needless to say, I was not invited back.

Step three: Don't mess it up. This is by far the most difficult of the three to put into practice and the one that creates the ugliest disasters when not strictly followed. I could tell you story after story of well-meaning outsiders who decided that the natives were doing things all wrong and needed correction. But I won't, because I suspect you know plenty of your own stories. To paraphrase the old saying: Oh, what a tangled mess we mix, when we apply a foreign fix.

We tried our best to follow the Firestones' guidelines because the strategy had obviously worked. Homer and Elvira managed to launch not one but two exceptionally successful church planting movements during their career in Bolivia. The first eventually outgrew its parent denomination in the U.S. Not bad for showing up with no plan.

By the time Barbara and I showed up, the second movement that the Firestones launched had become the largest and fastest growing national church in our denomination in Latin America. Over the next two decades, we watched *La Iglesia de Dios Reformada* triple in size. Accurate statistics were difficult to collect, but a fair guesstimate would be 12 to 15 thousand baptisms and approximately 160 new congregations planted.

Understand, I conducted a relative handful of the baptisms and Barbara and I did not plant one single church. We had our hands full just trying to keep up with our Bolivian coworkers.

Florencio Colque was one of those coworkers. He was, like all leaders in the Bolivian church, a tentmaker. Weekdays he operated bulldozers and road graders for the Highway Department to support his family. Weekends, he showed up to present the gospel at *juntas* [HOON-tahs], rural camp meetings that feature all-day music and Bible teaching. One of the most intelligent men I have ever known, Florencio spoke three languages fluently, although he never made it past the second grade.

We spent a good deal of time together traveling to juntas and I often heard Florencio present the gospel *a la boliviana*. I remember one sermon in particular.

"We learned from our grandfathers to walk a certain road," he told the assembled campesinos. "They told us 'You must worship this rock, this spring, this mountain peak.' When we asked them why this was, they said, 'Because this is the teaching we received from our grandfathers.'

"Then, humble men came to us with the gospel and spoke to us in a way that we could understand and believe. Now we have come out of darkness. Now we have entered the light. Now we worship God in spirit and in truth."

This stuck with me because I believe it explains the essence of why Andean peoples are coming to Jesus in great numbers. It has to do with freedom from fear.

Fear incited the persecution of the earliest Christian believers in the Andes. For instance, when Florencio and his family first turned to Jesus, their neighbors beat them up and threatened to kill them if they did not return to the old religion. This was because the rituals they inherited from their grandfathers were designed to appease the demons and pay homage to the gods of nature. Failure to perform these rites invited severe punishments. The village might suffer a plague, or the crops might fail, or the livestock would stop reproducing.

I once witnessed up close and personal the interplay between fear and freedom and I remember it as if it were yesterday. A middle-aged campesino, I will call him Pedro, came up to me one day at a junta and told me he had just been baptized. I congratulated him for it.

"Now I need to clean up my house," Pedro said earnestly, "and I want your help."

No one had ever made this sort of request before. I thought it kind of odd and was inclined to brush it off. But Tomas and Felix, two of our Bolivian coworkers, were standing nearby and overheard the conversation. They nodded their heads as if understanding perfectly what Pedro wanted and agreed to help him.

"What's this about?" I asked Tomas. "What does he want us to do?"

"It's kind of hard to explain," he said, "but you'll see."

So, on the appointed day we showed up at Pedro's village with no plan and me wondering what kind of mess I had gotten myself into. The place was typical of Andes farm

Home in the Llajta

communities, scattered adobe houses adorned with talismans fixed like lightning rods on the rooftops. These are *Ojos de Dios* [Eyes of God] and serve to ward off evil spirits. The homeowners likely had buried dried llama fetuses under their front doors, as well, a common custom to gain favor with Pachamama, the goddess of the earth.

A beaming Pedro met us and led the way to the side of his house. He explained that when he built the place, he had buried a Devil's

Banquet in the adobe wall as protection against wandering demons. Should one pass by when hungry and not find anything to eat, he might get angry and exact revenge.

The Devil's Banquet symbolized the apprehension that Pedro had lived with every day before he met Jesus. But now he was no longer intimidated by demons and devils and he wanted to be rid of this symbol of the old fears. He handed us a pick and shovel and pointed out where to start digging.

I half expected Tomas and Felix to lead us in a solemn ceremony before uncovering the Devil's Banquet, something akin to those scenes in Hollywood movies with spooky background music meant to break the spell of ancient gods. But nothing doing. The two were cracking jokes as they attacked the wall.

In minutes they had pried the banquet out of the adobe and I got my first look at the thing. It consisted of a three-foot length of log, hollowed out and a lid cut into one side. We lifted that off and peered at the hard candies, ears of corn, communion wafers and other stale edibles packed inside.

"Look here, these demons didn't eat a thing!" Tomas snickered. "And no wonder, this stuff is garbage!"

"You really expect a self-respecting demon to eat this junk?"

Pedro looked puzzled. His Devil's Banquet offered pretty much the standard fare because he had purchased it from certified witches who knew the correct ingredients.

Felix clasped a hand on his shoulder and winked. "Brother, if you wanna pacify the Devil, you had better provide some better eats. Otherwise, don't bother!"

Pedro smiled sheepishly and joined in the mirth. It turned out to be the funniest house cleaning party I have ever been invited to.

After some refreshments, we said goodbye to Pedro, carried off the hollow log and made us a bonfire on the way home. As we watched the flames turn the banquet to ash, it dawned on me that this was precisely the right way to assault the gates of Hell. If Jesus is truly Lord, why shouldn't we cast out demons with whoops and hollers, instead of apprehension and dread?

Jesus is Lord, of course. He scatters the darkness, sets captives free, opens blind eyes and gives an entirely new start in life to anyone who trusts Him. And He doesn't stop there.

Before He left earth, he told the apostles that he was going to build a splendid home for all His friends, "a house not made by hands, eternal in the Heavens."

To me that sounds like a Place even better than the Llajta,

Sites unseen

Barbara, Ben, Molly, Lindsey and I finished the Epic Journey with a safe arrival in Cochabamba. Several friends followed our progress through the blogs we posted along the way. In fact, the interest in the Epic surpassed expectations. Fetching feedback from readers ultimately inspired me to put this book together in an attempt to motivate more of our friends to do overland travel in Latin America.

Often our blog readers asked about places that we did NOT pass through on the trip from Indiana to Bolivia. Of course, these are myriad. It would take a lifetime to travel to all the exotic destinations and intriguing points of interest in the part of the world known as Latin America.

That said, I decided to include a sort of Epilogue to this book. The following chapters take us to three more places in South America that definitely rank as Bucket List To-Dos. I call them *Sites Unseen*, because we did not actually pass through them on the Epic.

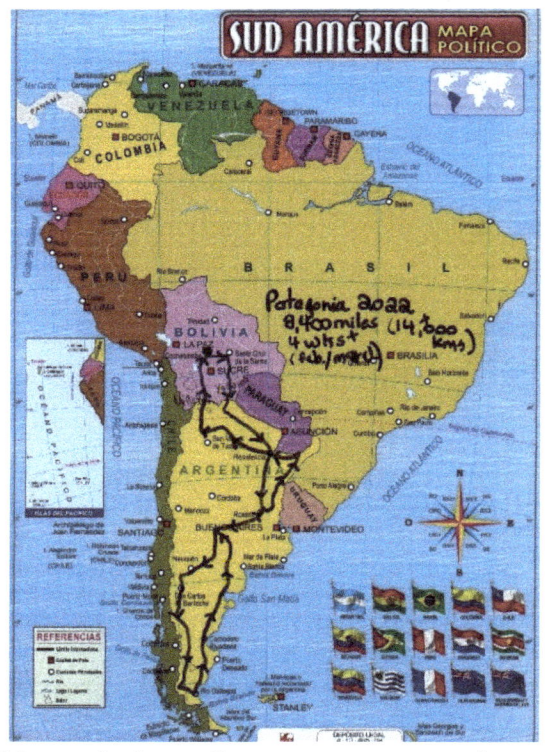

Nevertheless, I can assure you that our family has traveled these stretches of road one or more times over the course of our life in Latin America. And yes, we experienced adventure and wonder at every mile. Hope you can come along and share the ride.

Patagonia

I have had several wonderful opportunities in my life to take road trips from the Mississippi River across North America's Great Plains, over its western mountain ranges and deserts and on to the Pacific coast. It is roughly the same route that the 49ers took to the California Gold Rush and migrant farmers followed to Oregon. The crossing never fails to inspire awe for those hardy travelers of the 1800s who completed the journey in covered wagons, or on a horse, or on foot.

One of the most astonishing places a traveler might come to on this westward trek is Lake Tahoe. A wonder of nature perched 6,200 feet above sea level on the Nevada-California border, Tahoe is the next largest body of freshwater in the United States after the Great Lakes and covers an area about the size of Washington, D.C. Stunning snow-capped mountains and evergreen forests surround its crystalline waters, creating vistas that dazzle the eye and inspire the soul.

A trip across South America's Patagonia offers a similar encounter with geography. Flat, featureless plains stretch westward from Atlantic beaches across Argentina to the foothills of the Andes mountains. Crossing these majestic peaks, you descend to the fertile valleys and forests of southern Chile before reaching the Pacific Ocean.

However, in contrast to the considerable distance one must cover to cross the North American West, traveling coast to coast across Patagonia is a snap. The Atlantic-to-Pacific route here covers only one-third the distance between Saint Louis and San Francisco. And that is at Patagonia's widest point. As the continent tapers southward, arid flatlands squeeze together with Andean peaks until the two fuse completely at the tip of Tierra del Fuego.

I should mention another contrast. Despite its smaller size, Patagonia contains not just one Lake Tahoe, but around three dozen. Most are surrounded by lush evergreen forests and offer stunning views of snow-capped mountains. The first one Barbara and I visited, Lake Nahuel Huapi, is about three times the size of Tahoe.

Like 99 percent of visitors to Patagonia, we did not travel east to west but north to south, which makes for a sizable trek. The round trip from our home in Bolivia covered 8,300 miles, almost equivalent to three trips across the U.S.A.

We did this in February 2022, at the tail end of the Covid 19 pandemic. International travel was just beginning to ramp up again and Argentine citizens had only recently been released from strict quarantine and social distancing rules. They made up the great majority of our fellow travelers, with just a smattering of European bikers and Asian tourists. As a result, we enjoyed light traffic on the highways, readily available accommodations and plenty of elbow room in public spaces.

We had been warned about Patagonia's penetrating cold and harsh winds. "Be careful opening your car doors," was one common caution. "The wind can literally tear them off the hinges." But this particular February--the equivalent to August in the northern hemisphere--offered only bright sunshine, warm temps and an occasional light breeze. Every day was pretty much paradise.

What enhanced the experience even more was traveling with our Argentine friends, Bernardo and Monica Fischer, who planned the itinerary and advised us on logistics. They even set up overnight stays along the way with cousins, aunts and uncles, who treated Barbara and me like family. Had we not tagged along with the Fischers, we would have missed many of the spectacular sights of Patagonia and much of the region's charm.

If you, like me, like to eat then you will thoroughly enjoy Argentina's edibles. We especially enjoyed Esquel's beef empanadas, hot and fresh and served by the dozen. Esquel, by the way, is where you can take a day trip on a charming turn-of-the-20th-century steam-powered train. An outdoor restaurant in Colonia Suiza serves a fabulous meal of meat and vegetables slow-cooked underground. This village, by the way, is just a stone's throw from Bariloche, the city that boasts the most stunning and recognizable panorama of Lake Nahuel Huapi. And don't pass up the fresh seafood on Comodoro Rivadavia's seafront. You will also want to stop at some of the many *churrasquerías* serving up world-famous Argentine steaks. Save room for the excellent ice cream and pastry shops you come across. None will disappoint.

Among the non-edible Patagonian charms that stood out was the La Asencion Sheep Station near the town of Los Antiguos, Argentina's "cherry capital." Built by Scottish ranchers on the shore of massive Lake Buenos Aires in the 1880s, La Asencion prospered until worldwide demand for wool declined after WW1 and many Patagonia sheep stations closed. Now a national park, La Asencion invites visitors to roam its restored barns and bunkhouses and camp on the lakeshore. Old photos in its small museum depict shipments of wool, piled to colossal heights on freight wagons with wheels taller than a man's head, rolling over Patagonia sagebrush.

Impressive as they are, Patagonia's man-made spectacles are dwarfed by the natural splendor that God created in this part of the world. From San Martin de los Andes and Chile's Araucania region at its northern extremity, to Cape Horn at its southern tip, Patagonia is pure, uninterrupted beauty.

Patagonia got its name from Ferdinand Magellan, who stopped here in 1520 on his historic voyage around the world. The explorer described the Native Americans living on the Atlantic coast at the time as large people who stood a head taller than the Europeans. His sailors called them "*patagones*" (pot-ah-GO-nes), literally "big feet" in Spanish. Cartographers subsequently labeled the land "Patagonia" on maps of the New World.

Magellan did not see any of Patagonia's majestic mountains until he had sailed down the flat Atlantic coast and reached Tierra del Fuego. The endless expanse of dry grass and low brush that covers eastern Patagonia features little in the way of scenery, except for plentiful herds of guanaco (wild cousins to the llama) and flocks of avestruz (cousins to the ostrich). The featureless

Southward Bound

geography is great for building highways, however. Route 40, the primary north-south roadway, evokes the same romance and adventure for Argentines as Route 66 does for Americans.

Our travels took us as far south as Perito Moreno Glacier, which attracts more visitors than any other glacier in South America. By the way, unlike most glaciers in the world today, Perito Moreno is not shrinking, thanks to constant inflow from the Southern Patagonian Ice Field. The world's third largest reserve of freshwater, the Ice Field feeds 47 other glaciers in Argentina and Chile, including the Bruggen Glacier, the largest in the southern hemisphere outside Antarctica.

The most arresting scenery on the trip was Mount Fitz Roy, a jagged granite peak jutting out of the north end of the Patagonian Ice Field near the village of Chalten. First scaled in 1952, just one year before climbers reached the top of Mount Everest, Fitz Roy continues to attract world-class climbers, bolstering Chalten's

Patagonia

economy and keeping the tiny village on the map..

The famous peak is named for Robert Fitzroy, the British seaman who captained the HMS Beagle from 1831 to 1836 on its historic voyage to the Galapagos Islands with Charles Darwin aboard. Years later, when Darwin published his book *Origin of the Species*, Fitzroy publicly lamented his own part in introducing evolutionary theory to the world. A deeply religious man, Fitzroy had tried, unsuccessfully, to establish a Christian mission on the South American continent.

This feat would eventually be accomplished by another British sea captain, Allen Gardiner. Commissioned as an officer in the Royal Navy in 1823, he had little interest in Christianity until, on a voyage from Cape Town to Asia, a serious personal crisis prompted him to seek and find Jesus.

Following the death of his wife in 1834, Gardner dedicated himself exclusively to missionary work. He went to live among the Zulu of South Africa and was one of the founders of the city of Durban.

He then cast his eye upon South America, arriving in Patagonia in 1842 on a ship from the Falkland Islands. Intrigued by the native peoples in Tierra del Fuego, he returned to England and organized a team of seven men to carry the gospel to them. The band included Richard Williams, a surgeon, ship's carpenter Joseph Irwin, John Maidment, a Bible teacher, and three fishermen from Cornwall. They invested an initial donation of £700 in two 26-foot boats, stocked them with provisions and in 1850 sailed for Patagonia aboard the *Ocean Queen*.

After three months at sea, the missionaries reached Tierra del Fuego and off-loaded their boats on Picton Island, a cold, windswept spot inhabited by the Yahgan people. Staunchly hostile to outsiders, the natives prevented the men from leaving the beach and sheltering inland. The men were forced to live on the provisions they had brought with them. When supplies eventually ran out, the men began to die of starvation, one by one.

Gardiner himself was the last to succumb. When a relief ship finally reached Picton Island a year later, they found him clutching his diary, in which he had written a final entry on September 6, 1851. It read, *"Oh Lord, may we be your instruments in beginning this great work. But if it seems good to you to take us out of the way, or if we have to perish, I ask that you would lift up others and send them as workers to this harvest. Grant that this might succeed for the manifestation of your glory and grace. Nothing is too hard for thee..."*

There, the water-stained diary ended.

When news of the sacrifice of the seven brave men reached England, donations began pouring in to mission headquarters in Brighton. Charles Darwin himself is said to have contributed to the cause. The substantial funding enabled the mission to build and outfit its own sailing ship, the schooner *Allen Gardiner*.

Hundreds of men and women presented themselves to serve as missionaries. In 1856, the late captain's only son, Alan Gardiner Jr., sailed from England on the schooner named for his father to establish a successful mission in Lota, Chile.

Patagonia

Eventually, the movement became known as the South American Mission Society. Its workers planted churches and opened schools across the continent, many of which still thrive. Their efforts helped prepare the soil for a much larger wave of evangelical missionaries who began arriving in South America around the turn of the twentieth century. Their numbers increased substantially following WW2, reinforced with military veterans and energized by the vigorous Pentecostal movement.

Around the middle of the last century, Latin American evangelicals witnessed the beginning of a revival that continues to sweep the continent. According to British sociologist David Martin, 400 new believers come to Jesus in Latin America *every hour*. Today, the church in Latin America sends out more missionaries to other continents than those arriving from abroad.

I find it remarkable that all this began on a cold, lonely, wind-swept beach in Patagonia with seven desperate men whose plans appeared to have utterly failed.

It just goes to show that nothing is too hard for God.

Atacama Desert

We were halfway through a two-day crossing of the Atacama, the world's driest desert, and the hood on our pickup truck was rattling and shaking so fiercely I feared it might fly off and come through the windshield at us. Barbara and I agreed that we must get help, and urgently. But where, in the midst of this desolation? We prayed, as we customarily do when no other options are available.

The rattling had been a recurring nuisance ever since a front-end collision that our truck had suffered more than a year earlier. (I won't mention who was driving, in the interests of marital harmony.) The pickup came back from the body shop in reasonably good shape, except for the jiggly hood. It steadily worsened, so we had the shop repair it again, and again.

When it came time to leave on a three-week family road trip to the south of Chile, we decided that a jiggly hood was not a reasonable cause for canceling the long-anticipated adventure. So, early one morning before Christmas, we sallied forth with our four kids and some cautious optimism.

The first 3,000 miles were smooth enough and we enjoyed uninterrupted travel all the way down to the

Atacama Desert

phenomenally beautiful Lake District. (Just how beautiful is the Lake District? See photos in the previous chapter, *Patagonia*.)

The noxious rattle returned as we neared Santiago on the back haul. With 1,500 miles to go and the Atacama lying between us and home, I bit the bullet and took the truck in once again for therapy. Next morning, the repair shop pronounced it fixed, so with cautious optimism we pointed the hood north toward Bolivia.

Perhaps it was the Atacama wind that undid the repair shop's patch job, but by day two the hood was rattling and jiggling as never before. It was just after the "amen" to our desperate prayer that Barbara spotted a lonely gas station on the horizon. We did not pass it, as I customarily do. (But I won't go into that, again in the interests of marital harmony.)

"Well, we can't fix your hood here," the lean, sunburned attendant said. "But I know a couple fellas in town who can."

The "town" he pointed us to was a mining settlement at the bottom of a bowl-shaped canyon below the desert surface. As we descended from the rim into the depths below, I had sudden flashbacks from Star Wars movies. We were not in South America anymore. This was the planet Tatooine. I half expected Luke Skywalker to zip by in his land speeder.

We located the two fellas, who were even leaner and more sunburned than the guy at the gas station. They seemed gently amused by my description of the hood shake. "Let's have a look," said one, with an elfish twinkle in his eye.

His first move was to sprawl spread-eagle across the hood and wiggle around a bit. Then he jumped off, sprung the latch and gazed at the hood's insides.

"Yeah, I think we can fix you up," he said with a nod. "But it's gonna take a while. Why don't you go down the street and get some ice cream while you wait."

I confess I had serious qualms about walking away from our truck, especially after watching this stranger wallow around on its ailing bonnet. But then ice cream with Barbara and the kids in the middle of the world's driest desert sounded like a good idea. Surprisingly, the ice cream was very good. And in a surprisingly short time the man came by to say the truck was ready to go.

Of course, I looked over the entire hood carefully. It did seem, let's say, more settled than before. "What do I owe you?" I asked the two fellows.

"Not a thing," Twinkly Eyes said. "Didn't need any parts, and it hardly took any time at all."

"Oh, but sir," I protested. "This is a serious problem. Please, let me pay you."

The two exchanged amused glances. "Nah, we don't need anything," the man said with another elfish grin. "Just have a nice trip home."

And you know what? We did. That hood never jiggled once, all the way across the Atacama. In fact, the noxious shake never returned as long as we owned the truck. The Tatooine mechanics had worked a miracle.

I would like to go back someday and thank them for saving our vacation, and probably our lives. But it's a long way down there and I wonder if I could even find that bowl-shaped canyon again. And if I did, I doubt the two fellows would still be there. I have even begun to suspect that they were really angels, the kind that disappear after working miracles for desperate travelers.

In fact, I sometimes wonder if the whole incident was just a mirage. After all, we were smack in the middle of the Atacama, and stranger things have happened in the world's driest desert.

Atacama Desert

Just how dry is the Atacama? Well, since 1570 when humans began measuring its rainfall, about 0.04 inch has fallen per year. That makes the Atacama roughly 50 times drier than Death Valley and much more parched than the great Sahara Desert, which averages a whopping three inches of annual precipitation.

There is one disclaimer to World's Driest Desert status that should be mentioned. Geographers have discovered that certain parts of Antarctica actually receive less precipitation than the Atacama. I say, okay, but that doesn't really count, because Antarctica has two great advantages going for it: ice and penguins.

What cannot be denied is that the Atacama ranks as one of the planet's longest deserts, and certainly the skinniest. According to official geographers, it stretches 1,354 miles from Copiapó, Chile, up to Ica, Peru. According to unofficial road trippers like myself, the Atacama runs another 900 miles further north, nearly to the border of Ecuador. Supposedly, the barren reaches of Peru's coastline comprise another desert called the Pampas de la Joya, but you couldn't tell it by me. It's all just miles and miles and miles of dry sand punctuated by drier rocks and ridges. Geographers have nicknamed it "Mars on Earth".

Whatever its true length, the desert's span is comparatively teeny. The Atacama occupies a narrow strip between the blue Pacific Ocean and the towering Andes mountains. Its widest west-to-east point, between Antofagasta and San Pedro de Atacama, covers a mere 140 miles.

Perhaps you are imagining the Atacama as a blistering inferno under a merciless sun. Well, sometimes and in some places. But fog and clouds often cover stretches of the desert for months at a time. Daytime temperatures average a comfortable 66 degrees Fahrenheit. This is due to the Pacific Ocean's Humbolt Current, an icy stream that flows north from Antarctica and acts as a natural air conditioner for the west coast of South America.

If you have never heard of the Atacama before now, I bet you have heard of the Nazca Lines. Mammoth works of art known as geoglyphs, the Lines are named for the ancient Nazca people who created them between 500 B.C. and 500 A.D. The geoglyphs consist of shallow incisions in the desert floor that form precise geometric shapes hundreds of yards long. Most are simple rectangles, circles or spirals. But many form cleverly stylized figures of people, plants and animals. The latter include a huge hummingbird, spider, fish, condor, heron, monkey, lizard, dog and cat.

The fact that the majority of these creatures do not naturally exist within hundreds of miles of the Atacama is just one of the mysteries surrounding the Nazca Lines. Another has to do with viewing them. The Lines are best seen from an airplane, which has led some observers to speculate that extra-terrestrials carved them with laser beams from hovering spacecraft.

It should be mentioned that the Nazca Lines are also clearly visible from the surrounding foothills and other high spots, including a three-story observation tower on the side of the Pan-American highway where road trippers can stop and get a peek. And with all due respect to the extra-terrestrial theorists, these are not the only prehistoric geoglyphs in the world. Similar mammoth art works are found in Australia, England and newly cleared areas of the Amazon rainforest, with no indication of laser beams or hovering spacecraft.

Surprising as it may seem, Atacama's Martian landscape attracts tens of thousands of tourists every year, including us. Our family has most frequently visited Iquique, Chile, which is only a day's drive from our home in Cochabamba. We go to enjoy time on its spacious beach, to shop in its immense duty-free zone, or catch a bus or plane south to Santiago.

Atacama Desert

We happened to be there once on a Sunday and decided to attend services at a Pentecostal church, primarily because we had discovered that, in the 1940s, Pentecostal Christians from Iquique had visited Bolivia. Thanks to their preaching, a handful of families in Oruro came to faith in Christ. Some years later, these same families founded the Bolivian church movement that we serve as missionaries. I was curious to see if some sort of similarity existed between our two faith communities.

Surprisingly, it did. The auditorium in Iquique was packed with several hundred solemn but ardent worshippers, who sang every verse of every hymn at full volume. Prayers were offered by the entire assembly, all together and also at full volume. We heard not one, but three sermons, each delivered by a volunteer preacher from the congregation. When it came time for the offering, no collection plates circulated. Instead, everybody lined up to file past two large baskets down front and drop in their money, while singing yet another hymn at full volume. We felt right at home.

I should mention that neither Barbara nor I are Pentecostal Christians. Like millions of non-Roman Catholics living in Latin America, we refer to ourselves as *evangélicos* ("evangelicals" in English). But on our very first trip to Chile, we learned that the country is a standout exception to this rule. The term "evangélicos" elicited blank stares and timid questions from the Christians we encountered. Once we clarified our basic beliefs and relationship to Jesus, the Chileans would explain that they were, in fact, the same kind of Christians as us. But in Chile, they had always called themselves *pentecostales*.

This peculiarity harks back to 1902 and a Methodist missionary named Willis C. Hoover. Soon after students at a Methodist Bible college in Kansas, U.S.A., experienced a spiritual revival they considered to be a modern Pentecost (See Acts, Chapter 2), Hoover began encouraging his fellow Methodists in Valparaíso and Santiago to seek the gifts of the Holy Spirit. A similar revival broke out and soon Methodist congregations in Chile were singing at full volume, praying out loud, shouting and speaking in tongues, in church no less.

This kind of behavior, as well as the theological views underlying it, were uncharacteristic of Methodists. In 1910, matters reached a head and the Chileans broke from their mother denomination to form the Methodist Pentecostal Church.

Unlike the vast majority of church splits, this one opened the door to unbridled growth. The Methodist Pentecostals grew so quickly, in fact, that they soon became the largest non-Catholic church in Chile. They kept growing and eventually spawned Latin America's original megachurch.

The Jotabeche Methodist Pentecostal Church on Alameda Avenue in Santiago is considered the granddaddy of megachurches in the Americas. So, years ago when I found myself in Santiago on a free-lance reporting trip, I made sure to visit a Sunday evening service there. The experience was so mind-boggling I wrote about it the next day in a FAX to the family back home. (Yes, a FAX. Email was still a novelty at the time.)

19 April, 1993
Dear Barbara, Sarah, Benjo, Molly and Carmen,

How are you all doing? I have had a good trip so far. Weather is the pits, though. Rain, gray skies, cool temps. Just what you hate, Sweetheart.

Visited Chile's largest church last night, the Methodist Pentecostal Church in Jotabeche. 15,000 in attendance, about one-fifth of the total membership, they told me. Could not speak with the bishop, Javier Vasquez, but had a nice chat with his press secretary--imagine! He let me take pictures from the choir loft during the service.

I miss all of you lots. Keep me in your prayers, as I will you. Hugs and kisses all around, Dave/Daddy.

Lest you suspect my FAX of containing typos or exaggerated stats, let me give some context. At the time of my visit, the 16,000-seat

Atacama Desert

Jotabeche auditorium was larger than any church building in the United States. Its choir loft was roomy enough to accommodate the congregation's 2,000-voice choir and the several hundred guitarists, accordionists and mandolin players who assembled every service to accompany the hymns.

Despite its size, Jotabeche's building could not accommodate the congregation's 80,000 members all at once, so the church instituted an attendance rotation system. Worshippers had permission to come to an Alameda Avenue service once a month. Otherwise, they met in smaller "class meetings" led by Bishop Vazquez's many assistants. Class meetings typically drew from 500 to 3,000 participants. A few class meetings had built their own auditoriums. At this writing, 30 years after my visit to Jotabeche, the church is thought to be the second largest congregation in the world after the Yoido Full Gospel in Seoul, South Korea.

Jotabeche is not the only Pentecostal church in Chile that has experienced exponential growth. The movement has so captivated the country that two-thirds of all non-Catholic Christians there identify themselves as pentecostales. The Pew Research Center calls Chile the most "pentecostalized" society in Latin America. Congregations have sprung up from Punta Arenas at the continent's southern tip, to the Lake District, to the immense Central Valley and as far north as, well, Iquique and beyond.

Which leads me to believe that if I ever do come across those two fellows who repaired the jiggly hood on our pickup truck years ago in the middle of the world's driest desert, it would turn out that they are not angels after all. More likely, they are pentecostales.

Inca heartland

I am told there are specific moments in a man's life when he faces his own mortality. One of them is the first time he must ask one of his children to do something for him that he cannot do for himself. That moment came for me on the Inca Trail about 200 yards shy of the summit of Warmi Wañusqa Pass, which is just shy of 14,000 feet.

The year was 2000. I was hiking to Machu Picchu, the famous Lost City of the Inca, with Sarah and Ben, teenagers at the time. By day two of the trek, thin Andes air and steep climbing had combined to add roughly 500 pounds to my backpack. I could not tote the thing one step further. That was the moment when Ben, who had already summited Warmi Wañusqa, came bounding back down and said, "Hey Dad, need some help?" Did I ever.

In spite of the paternal instinct to hide weakness from one's offspring, I gratefully let Ben slide the pack off my drooping shoulders. He carried it to the top with no special effort, while I staggered behind, gulping air to keep from passing out. To ease my embarrassment, I reminded myself that we had raised Ben and Sarah in the Andes and therefore their lungs and legs were attuned to altitude. Indeed, Ben could nearly keep pace with the Peruvian porters who carried the food and camping gear for our party of 16 trekkers in bulging burlap bags strapped to their backs all day long, at a trot.

"Warmi Wañusqa" means "Dead Woman" in Quechua, and I can think of no place more appropriately named. It is the highest point on the Inca Trail. From there the trail descends steadily to Machu Picchu over stone steps--about three billion, I think, though I admit I lost count-- hewed out by the ancient Incas themselves.

If you have ever contemplated putting the Inca Trail on your Bucket List, let me strongly encourage you to do so. The experience is, well, breathtaking. And the sense of satisfaction upon arriving under your own steam at a magnificent destination famous the world over endures for years afterward. But take heed, along the way you may come face to face with your own mortality.

The Inca emperor Pachacuti finished construction of Machu Picchu sometime around 1450 and built the Trail linking it to Cusco so that he could spend winter months and religious holidays in the secluded citadel. Along the route, he created *tambos* (guest houses) spaced at intervals of one day's hike. Local farmers kept the tambos stocked with blankets and provisions so that, unlike modern trekkers, the Inca and his entourage of nobles and soldiers were never burdened with backpacks. Pretty smart, eh?

These guys were very smart. The Incas studied the stars in order to accurately track the seasons and expertly managed soil and water resources in order to maximize crop yields. Along the Inca Trail you will find stone baths fed by springs whose temperature and flow remain constant year-round, and evidently have remained constant since the time of Pachacuti. Remnants of Cusco's city water system still survive, too, its pipes, tanks and valves engineered entirely from stone.

Cusco itself was engineered from stone. When you get a close look at its major public buildings--the temples of Korichancha, the Inca palaces and the imposing hilltop fortress of Sacsayhuaman--you realize that the Inca were not just smart, they were flat-out geniuses.

They built to last. The granite and limestone walls of these structures fit together so tightly a razor blade cannot slide between the joints. They have remained immovable through literally centuries of earthquakes. Did I mention that the Incas did not use mortar?

Archaeologists are at a loss to explain just how these stones were milled to such precision. One thing is for sure, they did not come off an assembly line. No two are alike, many have multiple corners and edges and fit together like a jigsaw puzzle. Some of the stones in the Sacsayhuaman fortress are the size of small houses and weigh tens of tons. Modern engineers are still trying to figure out how the fort's builders transported these monsters

Inca Heartland

22 miles over hill and dale from the site where they quarried them. Did I mention that the Incas did not use wheels?

A hike on the Inca Trail will show you why Pachacuti and his entourage did not bother with wheeled conveyance. Two legs can handle the steep terrain far better than a wagon, and if you need four legs to tote cargo, nothing suits the Andes better than the sure-footed llama.

Parts of the Inca Trail pass through the Sacred Valley. This narrow, 100-mile stretch of flat, fertile farmland flanking the Urubamba River is at the center of the Inca heartland. Ancient stone villages and ceremonial sites are scattered throughout the valley and on the steep slopes surrounding it. The most imposing of these is the massive Ollanta Tambo fortress that straddles a choke point in the valley and guards the final stretch of the road to Machu Picchu.

The last morning on the Trail, we arose in pre-dawn darkness to hike the few remaining miles to the Gate of the Sun, a spot several hundred feet above Machu Picchu where we waited for the sun to rise. This is a tradition among trekkers and was probably how the Incas themselves arranged their arrival. It happened to be Ben's 15th birthday, so 150 fellow trekkers sang to him. When we finished, an Aussie accented voice said, "Hey mates, t'day is Second of July, right? Well then, it's my birthday, too!" So, we sang a second round.

Then the sun rose, and as it did, its first rays conspicuously lit up the *Intihuatana*. This ritual stone carved out of a knoll in the middle of the citadel attracts subterranean rays of cosmic energy that flow to it from the cardinal points of the earth. At least, that is what a couple of starry-eyed young women from New York City had told us a few nights earlier at a cybercafé in Cusco. They said they had come to Peru to get in touch with the cosmos and had hired a tour guide who would take them to Machu Picchu and connect them directly to this cosmic energy source.

Be aware, in the unregulated tourist industry of Cusco you can find all manner of tour guides who, for a price, will tell you whatever you want to hear about the mysteries of Lost City. Fortunately, our guide was not one of them. When we descended from the Gate of the Sun to

Intihuatana, he rendered a less, um, Aquarian, explanation of its importance.

"Maybe somebody has told you about rays of cosmic energy that flow to this place from the four corners of the earth," he said, adding something that sounded like "patent nonsense, "but I can't remember the precise phrase in Spanish.

"See that small hole drilled into the west side of the stone?" he continued. "Astronomers have discovered that the shadow of the stone's opposite corner falls precisely on that spot on the day of the winter solstice. Once they established that date, the Incas could compose an accurate calendar, year after year, with no margin of error." Ah ha!

Did I mention that the Incas were smart guys? Oh yeah, I did. I will let you make up your own mind about the folks who theorize about rays of cosmic energy.

The Inca Trail runs smack through the middle of the Inca Heartland. That fact is reason enough to put it on your Bucket List because the Heartland lay at the very center of the vast Inca Empire.

At its zenith, the Inca Empire was the largest ever established in pre-Columbian America. It encompassed most of the present-day countries of Ecuador, Peru and Bolivia, and stretched into northern Chile and Argentina. The empire's population was twice that of Spain's at the time. The Inca trade language, Quechua, became South America's most

Inca Heartland

common tongue and is still spoken by millions.

One of the more extraordinary features of the Inca Empire had to do with longevity, which was fairly short as empires go. It took less than a century for the original Inca clan to break out of its ancestral homeland in the central Andes, conquer rival tribes and city states, forge them into a brilliant civilization, and then lose the entire enterprise to a handful of Spanish conquistadores.

Perhaps you have read how, in the year 1532, Francisco Pizarro and 177 soldiers of fortune captured the emperor Atahualpa, neutralized his entire army and assumed control of the empire. Many different versions exist about how that actually happened. The Incas left no written records because they did not use writing. Spoken Quechua worked just fine for them. The Spaniards wrote stuff down, but it was such one-sided propaganda that it's hard to distinguish truth from fake news.

One of the more credible accounts I have heard came from a Peruvian friend who heard it from his grandfather. The story had been passed down to him through many generations of Inca ancestors. It goes like this.

As he lay dying, the Inca Huayna Kapac called his two sons, Atahualpa and Huáscar, to his bedside and told them of an alarming omen. Days before, Huayna Kapac had watched a flock of small birds attack a powerful hawk and kill it. "Just as those small birds killed the great hawk, so a weaker enemy is going to destroy us," he prophesied. "God is about to punish us for our sin."

"What sin is that?" his sons asked.

"We have forgotten the True God," Huayna Kapac said. "We've made for ourselves idols, which he abhors, and have fallen away from his laws. God has sent these men to kill you, rape your daughters and destroy our throne."

Neither Huáscar nor Atahualpa heeded their father's warning. After his death, they declared war on one another, which depleted their armies and divided patriotic loyalties. The conflict ended just as Pizarro arrived on the shores of Peru.

Evidently, Atahualpa understood something about the true God of which his father had spoken, because he issued orders not to attack Pizzaro's men. He thought they might be messengers sent from the Great Creator God, the one the Incas called *Viracocha*. One of the strangers even wore long robes like those described in the legends about Viracocha. This would have been the Dominican friar, Vicente de Valverde. Valverde's attire is probably what persuaded Atahualpa to grant the priest an audience.

At Pizarro's insistence, this interview took place in the village of Cajamarca. Pizarro had hidden his soldiers in buildings surrounding the village plaza. They poised there with weapons at ready as Atahualpa and his entourage arrived, unarmed. Atahualpa felt it sacrilegious to bring weapons to a meeting with a representative of Viracocha.

Carrying a cross and a Bible, Valverde approached the Inca. Through a Quechua interpreter, he told Atahualpa that it was God's will that he should submit to Emperor Charles I of Spain and join his own empire to the great brotherhood of Christian nations. A skeptical Atahualpa asked Valverde how he knew this was God's will. Valverde said that it was all contained in the Bible that he held in his hand.

Atahualpa, who had never seen a book before in his life, asked the Quechua interpreter how the Bible worked. The man said, "God speaks to him in the book." Atahualpa took the Bible from Valverde and held it to his ear. Hearing nothing, he tossed the book on the ground in disgust.

"If your God is in there, he must be very small," he said to Valverde. "My God can hold the universe in his hand!"

The Inca's contempt for the sacred Book convinced Valverde that he was a hardened infidel who would never willingly convert to Christianity. The priest turned away and Pizarro signaled his men to commence the attack.

"Wow!" I said to my Peruvian friend when he finished his story. "That sounds a lot like the account in the anthropology books I have come across. Have you read them?" I rattled off a few titles.

"No," he said. "But I would like to."

"Do you suppose your grandfather ever read them?"

He blinked. "My grandfather couldn't read."

I blinked back, realizing that we had just struck upon an axiom that serious journalists follow when reporting news. If two or more sources independently agree on the facts of an event, you can be confident that their information is very close to the truth. Close enough, at any rate, to go to press with the story.

The stories my Peruvian friend heard from his grandfather also validated a phenomenon that missionaries call "redemptive bridges." Gospel workers the world over have come across surprising links between ancient beliefs of indigenous peoples and the Scriptures. Mission researcher Hannah Sevedge Ahn, defines such links as "a practice or belief native to a given culture that distinctly parallels or illustrates the gospel."

In our years of missionary work, Barbara and I have witnessed the impact of redemptive bridges upon descendants of Inca culture. Let me give a couple examples.

First of all, unlike we post-moderns of European descent, Andean peoples display an acute sense of the Holy. They seem to understand right off the bat that God is pure and righteous and humans are not and that can be awkward.

Our Inca Trail guide explained, for instance, that when the Inca and his entourage reached the final tambo on the way to Machu Picchu, instead staying just overnight, they spent several days there in order to purify themselves. They repeatedly bathed in the tambo's spring-fed stone pools, carefully washed all their clothes, and spent hours each day in self-examination to expose bad behavior that might offend Viracocha. These rituals, they believed, rendered them worthy to enter the sacred environs of Machu Picchu.

This custom holds an uncanny resemblance to the procedures that God commanded Levitical priests to perform before entering Temple service (*See Numbers, chapter eight*). It also parallels a spiritual discipline that native Bolivian Christians observe nowadays. The first Sunday of every third month, they arise before dawn to ascend to a deserted mountaintop. There they spend the day in fasting and prayer, with their Bibles open before them, asking God to reveal His will. They call this exercise "Repentance."

Another redemptive bridge is what our mentor, Dr. Homer Firestone, called the Viracocha Complex. He defined the Complex as an expectation, ingrained in Andes culture. The Incas knew something about the Creator God because of what they observed in creation (*See Romans, chapter one*). But they also knew that what they knew was woefully incomplete. Their legends taught that someday messengers of the true God would show up and fill in the blanks. Then they would know all they needed to know in order to know the True God Himself.

The Viracocha Complex explains why, even today, Andean peoples expect credible information about God to come to them from outside their own environment, and from outsiders. I could cite dozens of examples of how the Complex acts as a bridge for the gospel, but I would rather you hear it straight for the horse's mouth, so to speak.

In the earlier chapter "Home in the Llajta," I introduced my long-time friend and coworker, Florencio Colque, a descendant of the Incas and one of the first men in his village to follow Jesus. I quoted one of his sermons to a Quechua congregation that started out like this:

"Our grandfathers told us, 'You must worship this spring, this rock, this mountain peak, because this is the teaching we have received from our grandfathers.' Then men came to us with the gospel and spoke to us so that we could understand and believe."

Florencio finished up by saying, "When I was a boy, I called my sheep. 'Baaa! Baaa!' I called and they listened. When they were certain it was me calling, they followed because they knew my voice. In the same way, we now recognize Jesus' voice from all the others and follow Him."

I know what you're thinking. "Okay, I get it, but this is nothing new. I've heard the same things about Jesus and the gospel all my life." Exactly. The gospel is the gospel the world over, and anybody can understand the story of redemption if they hear it in language they understand. We find that most people will acknowledge Jesus as their best friend if they can but recognize his voice.

This truth is precisely what motivated Homer Firestone and Florencio Colque to take the gospel to the descendants of the Inca. It is what motivates countless other missionaries and itinerant preachers the world over to do what they do. For my part, I consider it the most important enterprise being done on earth in our day.

Because sooner or later, the moment will come when all of us must face our own mortality.

This concludes *Southward Bound: The adventure and wonder of road trips through Latin America*. Thanks for joining us! We hope you have enjoyed the ride and wish you joyous travels on all of your own epic journeys.

God bless you!

Inca Heartland